BUZZ WORDS

POEMS ABOUT INSECTS

EDITED BY
HAROLD SCHECHTER
AND KIMIKO HAHN

EVERYMAN'S LIBRARY
POCKET POETS

Alfred A. Knopf   New York   London   Toronto

THIS IS A BORZOI BOOK

PUBLISHED BY ALFRED A. KNOPF

This selection by Harold Schechter and Kimiko Hahn
first published in Everyman's Library, 2021
Copyright © 2021 by Everyman's Library

A list of acknowledgments to copyright owners appears
at the back of this volume.

All rights reserved. Published in the United States by Alfred A.
Knopf, a division of Penguin Random House LLC, New York, and
in Canada by Penguin Random House Canada Limited, Toronto.
Distributed by Penguin Random House LLC, New York. Published
in the United Kingdom by Everyman's Library, 50 Albemarle
Street, London W1S 4BD and distributed by Penguin Random
House UK, 20 Vauxhall Bridge Road, London SW1V 2SA.

www.randomhouse/everymans
www.everymanslibrary.co.uk

ISBN 978-1-101-90826-6 (US)
978-1-84159-821-5 (UK)

A CIP catalogue record for this book is available
from the British Library

Typography by Peter B. Willberg

Typeset in the UK by Input Data Services Ltd, Isle Abbotts, Somerset

Printed and bound in Germany
by GGP Media GmbH, Pössneck

CONTENTS

SPARKLERS AND SWOOPERS

GLIDERS

CRAWLERS

STINGERS, BITERS, AND SUCKERS

FOREWORD

Scientists estimate that, at any time, there are ten quin-tillion insects on the earth – or, to put the figure in more comprehensible terms, more than 200 million in-sects for every human being. This is a sobering statistic to contemplate for the legions who share the sentiment expressed in the Book of Leviticus: "All flying insects that creep on all fours shall be an abomination to you." It is, however, a useful reminder of the extent to which our world is made up of such creatures. And since (to quote Edward Hirsch's *A Poet's Glossary*), "the natural world has been one of the recurring subjects of poetry, frequently the primary one, in every age and every country," it is no surprise that there is a rich body of verse on the creeping, scuttling, stinging things – *Hexapoda*, to use the proper entomological term – with which we share our planet.

That insects can serve as a suitable subject for poetry would come as no surprise to any child familiar with the various nursery rhymes about lady bugs, glow worms, and spiders (nitpickers like to point out that, strictly speaking, spiders aren't bugs, but try telling that to Little Miss Muffet). Cultures other than our own have centuries-old traditions of insect verse. In China – where noblewomen of the Tang dynasty kept crickets in gold cages to serenade them at night – countless songs were written in praise of these "insect musicians." The haiku masters of Japan similarly composed thousands of poems not only about crickets but also about grasshoppers, cicadas, fireflies, dragonflies, and butterflies, along with such less prepossessing bugs as houseflies, fleas, and mosquitoes.

In the West, poems about insects date back to the ancient Greek collection known as the *Garland*, compiled by the poet-anthologist Meleager. In later centuries, insects feature so frequently in British works from the Elizabethan period onward that scholars have produced entire entomological studies of the literature (most notably, Pearl Faulkner Eddy's "Insects in English Poetry," subtitled "Bugs in Books," a delightful forty-page survey that appeared in two successive issues of *The Scientific Monthly* in 1931). Insects appear in American literature beginning with the work of Philip Freneau – aka "The Father of American Poetry" – and extending to the sequence of bee poems in Sylvia Plath's *Ariel* and up to the present moment.

Though his métier was prose, not poetry, the great French entomologist, Jean-Henri Fabre, wrote so brilliantly on his subject that Victor Hugo dubbed him the "Homer of Insects" and Provençal poet Frédéric Mistral campaigned for his nomination for the 1911 Nobel Prize in Literature. Addressing the reader in his 1918 book, *The Life and Love of the Insect*, Fabre asks, "What is the use of this history, what the use of all this minute research?" and responds with characteristic wit and eloquence: "I well know that it will not produce a fall in the price of pepper, a rise in that of crates of rotten cabbages, or other serious events of this kind, which cause fleets to be manned and set people face to face intent upon one another's extermination. The insect does not aim at so much glory. It confines itself to showing us life in the inexhaustible variety of its manifestations; it helps us decipher in some small measure the obscurest book of all, the book of ourselves."

Though the poems in this volume vary widely in regard to style, tone, genre, and theme, that recognition of the insect's significance to our lives informs them all.

Harold Schechter
Kimiko Hahn

INSECTARIUM

SLEEPING ON THE CEILING

It is so peaceful on the ceiling!
It is the Place de la Concorde.
The little crystal chandelier
is off, the fountain is in the dark.
Not a soul is in the park.

Below, where the wallpaper is peeling,
the Jardin des Plantes has locked its gates.
Those photographs are animals.
The mighty flowers and foliage rustle;
under the leaves the insects tunnel.

We must go under the wallpaper
to meet the insect-gladiator,
to battle with a net and trident,
and leave the fountain and the square.
But oh, that we could sleep up there. . . .

ELIZABETH BISHOP (1911–79)

BUGS IN A BOWL

Han Shan, that great and crazy, wonder-filled
Chinese poet of a thousand years ago, said:

We're just like bugs in a bowl. All day
going around never leaving their bowl.

I say, That's right! Every day climbing up
the steep sides, sliding back.

Over and over again. Around and around.
Up and back down.

Sit in the bottom of the bowl, head in your hands,
cry, moan, feel sorry for yourself.

Or. Look around. See your fellow bugs.
Walk around.

Say, Hey, how you doin'?
Say, Nice bowl!

INSECTS

Thou tiney loiterer on the barleys beard
And happy unit of a numerous herd
Of playfellows the laughing summer brings
Mocking the sunshine in their glittering wings
How merrily they creep and run and flye
No kin they bear to labours drudgery
Smoothing the velvet of the pale hedge rose
And where they flye for dinner no one knows
The dew drops feed them not – they love the shine
Of noon whose sun may bring them golden wine
All day theyre playing in their sunday dress
Till night goes sleep and they can do no less
Then in the heath bells silken hood they flie
And like to princes in their slumber lie
From coming night and dropping dews and all
In silken beds and roomy painted hall
So happily they spend their summer day
Now in the corn fields now the new mown hay
One almost fancys that such happy things
In coloured hoods and richly burnished wings
Are fairy folk in splendid masquerade
Disguised through fear of mortal folk affraid
Keeping their merry pranks a mystery still
Lest glaring day should do their secrets ill

JOHN CLARE (1793–1864)   21

From *URBAN TUMBLEWEED*

With daily commuters, an extra passenger
on the bus. Ladybug clinging to the window
didn't need to pay a fare.

From a distance, wrecked cars on the freeway
are crumpled toys, the helicopter
circling up above, a curious dragonfly.

You may wrap yourself in silk pajamas
after nibbling your coverlet,
chenille caterpillar lounging on a tender leaf.

Office memos send notice of ants invading
the sugar bowl kept in the coffee break room,
lost bees swarming in the stairwell.

When you complain about the worm
in your salad bowl, our server assures us,
"That is how you know the lettuce is organic."

Ninety-nine dashing dots crisscross
the walk, red ants converging on a spot where
someone's dropped a greasy bite of pepperoni.

Feeding on a single weed, its habitat
dwindling, can the caterpillar afford to be
so choosy with its appetite?

Folded cardboard tent-shaped trap
hanging among dark leaves of the lemon tree
to capture the galling Mediterranean fly.

Stone-ground flour from co-op bulk bins
brings dusty moths that hatch in my kitchen canister
and fly out when I want to bake biscuits.

On the porch, serenaded by a cricket choir –
so charming! Lying in bed, the chirp
of a single cricket – so annoying!

Inspired by swarms of oily insects: "If you
can't beat them, eat them," said the inventive
chef who created the locust pizza.

MISS SPIDER'S GUESTS

> "Can the Butterflies come to Miss Spider's Tea Party?"
> – International Playthings, Inc.

They swarm Miss Spider's Tea Party: Gnats, June
Beetles, Ladybugs, Flies. The Red Ants stress,
"Don't drop into a cup," meanwhile Moths moon
over bright candles on the cake. "Obsess

about details," instructs Miss Spider. Snake
glides across rug, hissing: "That point is moot.
You trap each guest inside your skein!" "The cake
is honey-sweet," buzz all the Wasps, "A beaut!"

May arrives late, fedora dipped like Garbo,
all feint and mystery. Will Ike now play
his cards, reveal his hand, gent or hobo?
They flutter, feast, and crawl, all night, all day.

Miss Firefly flashes a hefty rhinestone.
Mr. Bumblebee sports too much cologne.

THE BUTTERFLY'S BALL AND THE
GRASSHOPPER'S FEAST

Come, take up your hats, and away let us haste
To the Butterfly's ball and the Grasshopper's feast;
The trumpeter Gad-fly has summon'd the crew,
And the revels are now only waiting for you.

On the smooth-shaven grass by the side of the wood,
Beneath a broad oak that for ages has stood,
See the children of earth, and tenants of air,
For an evening's amusement together repair.

And there came the Beetle, so blind and so black,
Who carried the Emmet, his friend, on his back;
And there came the Gnat, and the Dragon-fly too,
And all their relations, green, orange, and blue.

And there came the Moth with her plumage of down,
And the Hornet with jacket of yellow and brown.
Who with him the Wasp, his companion, did bring;
They promised that evening to lay by their sting.

Then the sly little Dormouse peep'd out of his hole,
And led to the feast his blind cousin the Mole;
And the Snail, with his horns peeping out from his shell,
Came fatigued with the distance, the length of an ell.

A mushroom the table, and on it were spread
A Water-dock-leaf, which their table-cloth made;
The viands were various, to each of their taste,
And the Bee brought the honey to sweeten the feast.

With steps more majestic the Snail did advance,
And he promised the gazers a minuet dance;
But they all laughed so loudly he pulled in his head,
And went in his own little chamber to bed.

Then, as evening gave way to the shadows of night,
Their watchman, the Glow-worm, came out with
his light:
So home let us hasten, while yet we can see,
For no watchman is waiting for you or for me.

WINDOWS AND MIRRORS

Ladybug moving along a cast-iron chair –
translucent pink of a budding lotus
in the pond – you slide along
a botanical wall, recall someone

who stammered to avoid the army
and then could not undo his stutter.
A wasp lays eggs in a tarantula;
a gecko slips under the outdoor grill.

You bite into a deep-fried scorpion
on a skewer: when your father reached
for the inhaler, your mother
stopped breathing. Iridescent green

butterflies pinned to the wall –
a rainbow passing across an island –
striding past ants on a bougainvillea,
you find windows and mirrors

in the refractive index of time.
Tracks of clothes on the floor –
white plumeria on the grass –
hatched wasps consume the tarantula.

ARTHUR SZE (1950 –)   27

THE INSECT

I dreamed that we were sitting, a party of twenty, in a big room with open windows.

Among us were women, children, old men. . . . We were all talking of some very well-known subject, talking noisily and indistinctly.

Suddenly, with a sharp, whirring sound, there flew into the room a big insect, two inches long . . . it flew in, circled round, and settled on the wall.

It was like a fly or a wasp. Its body dirt-coloured; of the same colour too its flat, stiff wings; outspread feathered claws, and a head thick and angular, like a dragon-fly's; both head and claws were bright red, as though steeped in blood.

This strange insect incessantly turned its head up and down, to right and to left, moved its claws . . . then suddenly darted from the wall, flew with a whirring sound about the room, and again settled, again hatefully and loathsomely wriggling all over, without stirring from the spot.

In all of us it excited a sensation of loathing, dread, even terror. . . . No one of us had ever seen anything like it. We all cried: "Drive that monstrous thing away!" and waved our handkerchiefs at it from a distance . . . but no one ventured to go up to it . . . and when the insect began flying, every one instinctively moved away.

Only one of our party, a pale-faced young man, stared at us all in amazement. He shrugged his shoulders; he smiled, and positively could not conceive what had happened to us, and why we were in such a state of excitement. He himself did not see an insect at all, did not hear the ill-omened whirr of its wings.

All at once the insect seemed to stare at him, darted off, and dropping on his head, stung him on the forehead, above the eyes. ... The young man feebly groaned, and fell dead.

The fearful fly flew out at once. ... Only then we guessed what it was had visited us.

IVAN TURGENEV (1818–83)   29
TRANSLATED BY CONSTANCE GARNETT

WORKERS

BOMBING THE SWARM

This swarm of bees was hanging
from the branch of a tall tree,
a writhing mass that clung together
and swung down like a black bell.

One of the boys, can't remember who,
picked up an apple – it was late August –
51 or 52 – and hurled it into the nest:
it came apart in hunks, like a skull exploding,

then recomposed; but we kept hurling apples
and the swarm kept flying apart, flying together,
replay of a bullet entering a man's brain.
Looking back, I realize we couldn't stop,

neither could the bees, we had this frenzy.
That's when I learned how dangerous
I was – so that now when I walk in a field,
my shadow makes crickets hush

and birds fly away in alarm.

KURT BROWN (1944 – 2013)

THE ANT'S PLUNDER

When I stuck out my hand to grab the iron door handle, a hidden ant attacked my right index finger. I don't know if it pinched me with its pincers or bit me with its mouth. I don't know how it got so strong.

In an instant, it turned itself into a weapon. The pain was so great that I cursed this neither common nor rare 1.5–centimeter long ant. This may be the greatest achievement of its life: to cause a man such piercing pain.

Like the filament of a lightbulb, the six legs of an ant befit its existence. Its body, bright yellow in front and brown in back, is filled with liquid, like two water droplets fused together.

Two water droplets fused together to produce a will to live, a will to live that produces the pincers protruding from the ant's head. The ant and the crab both use pincers, which are differentiated only by their size.

In stabbing pain, I examine this ant.

In the throbs of pain the ant and I encounter each other. I never thought "the encounter between Man and World" of which Heidegger spoke would find form between me and ant. This ant lives to sting me; I live to curse it in pain.

The arc of my life hooks onto the arc of its life, which is kind of significant. Kill it? Easy. But it knew I couldn't. It scurried away, flustered, pretending to ignore my curses.

VIRGIL'S BEES

Bless air's gift of sweetness, honey
from the bees, inspired by clover,
marigold, eucalyptus, thyme,
the hundred perfumes of the wind.
Bless the beekeeper

                who chooses for her hives
a site near water, violet beds, no yew,
no echo. Let the light lilt, leak, green
or gold, pigment for queens,
and joy be inexplicable but *there*
in harmony of willowherb and stream,
of summer heat and breeze,
                  each bee's body
at its brilliant flower, lover-stunned,
strumming on fragrance, smitten.

                  For this,
let gardens grow, where beelines end,
sighing in roses, saffron blooms, buddleia;
where bees pray on their knees, sing, praise
in pear trees, plum trees; bees
are the batteries of orchards, gardens, guard them.

THE BEE

However keen may be your sting,
However fatal, yellow bee,
Over my basket I have draped
The merest dream of floating lace.

So prick that swelling gourd, my breast
Where Love is sleeping, or has died.
A little of myself will rise
Scarlet to plump, rebellious flesh!

A sudden pang is what I need:
A pain that quickens and is gone
I'd rather than this slumbering grief.

Illuminate my senses with
Your microscopic gold alarm
Without which Love slumbers or dies!

PAUL VALÉRY (1871–1945)   37
TRANSLATED BY NATHANIEL RUDAVSKY-BRODY

THE HUMBLE-BEE

Burly, dozing humble-bee,
Where thou art is clime for me.
Let them sail for Porto Rique,
Far-off heats through seas to seek;
I will follow thee alone,
Thou animated torrid-zone!
Zigzag steerer, desert cheerer,
Let me chase thy waving lines;
Keep me nearer, me thy hearer,
Singing over shrubs and vines.

Insect lover of the sun,
Joy of thy dominion!
Sailor of the atmosphere;
Swimmer through the waves of air;
Voyager of light and noon;
Epicurean of June;
Wait, I prithee, till I come
Within earshot of thy hum, –
All without is martyrdom.

When the south wind, in May days,
With a net of shining haze
Silvers the horizon wall,
And, with softness touching all,

Tints the human countenance
With a color of romance,
And, infusing subtle heats,
Turns the sod to violets,
Thou, in sunny solitudes,
Rover of the underwoods,
The green silence dost displace
With thy mellow, breezy bass.

Hot midsummer's petted crone,
Sweet to me thy drowsy tone
Tells of countless sunny hours,
Long days, and solid banks of flowers;
Of gulfs of sweetness without bound
In Indian wildernesses found;
Of Syrian peace, immortal leisure,
Firmest cheer, and bird-like pleasure.

Aught unsavory or unclean
Hath my insect never seen;
But violets and bilberry bells,
Maple-sap, and daffodels,
Grass with green flag half-mast high,
Succory to match the sky,
Columbine with horn of honey,
Scented fern, and agrimony,

Clover, catchfly, adder's-tongue
And brier-roses, dwelt among;
All beside was unknown waste,
All was picture as he passed.

Wiser far than human seer,
Yellow-breeched philosopher!
Seeing only what is fair,
Sipping only what is sweet,
Thou dost mock at fate and care,
Leave the chaff, and take the wheat.
When the fierce northwestern blast
Cools sea and land so far and fast,
Thou already slumberest deep;
Woe and want thou canst outsleep;
Want and woe, which torture us,
Thy sleep makes ridiculous.

WORKERS (ATTENDANTS)

Nights we lie beside her, our mouths
at her belly, counting

her breaths, the buzz, the gathering, long
done. We all began
inside her, like those lined up

inside her now, mere
idea of ourselves
unborn. We wash her body

ceaselessly, move our tongues
until all her hairs loosen. She

roams the brood, finds
another empty cell

& fills it. Morning comes &
she calms us, keeps us inside
until the dew burns off. This sodden

world. All winter
we huddled around her, kept her
warm. Those on the outside, those
farthest from her, died

first, their legs
gripped the others like a shawl.

NICK FLYNN (1960–) 41

ODE TO THE BEEKEEPER
for Stephanie Smith

who has taken off her veil
and gloves and whispers to the bees
in their own language, inspecting the comb-thick
frames, blowing just so when one or the other alights
on her, if she doesn't study it first – the veins
feeding the wings, the deep ochre
shimmy, the singing – just like in the dreams
that brought her here in the first place: dream
of the queen, dream of the brood chamber,
dream of the desiccated world and sifting
with her hands the ash and her hands
ashen when she awoke, dream of honey
in her child's wound, dream of bees
hived in the heart and each wet chamber
gone gold. Which is why, first,
she put on the veil. And which is why,
too, she took it off.

LIKE AN ANT CARRYING HER BITS
OF LEAF OR SAND

Like an ant carrying her bits of leaf or sand,
the poem carries its words.
Moving one, then another, into place.

Something in an ant is sure where these morsels
    belong,
but the ant could not explain this.
Something in a poem is certain where its words
    belong,
but the poet could not explain this.

All day the ant obeys an inexplicable order.
All day the poet obeys an incomprehensible demand.

The world changes or does not change by these
    labors;
the geode peeled open gives off its cold scent or
    does not.
But that is no concern of the ant's, of the poem's.

The work of existence devours its own unfolding.
What dissolves will dissolve –
you, reader, and I, and all our quick angers and
    longings.

The potato's sugary hunger for growing larger.
The unblinking heat of the tiger.

No thimble of cloud or stone that will not vanish,
and still the rearrangements continue.

The ant's work belongs to the ant.
The poem carries love and terror, or it carries
     nothing.

"THERE WAS AN OLD MAN IN A TREE"

There was an Old Man in a tree,
Who was horribly bored by a Bee;
When they said, "Does it buzz?"
He replied, "Yes, it does!
It's a regular brute of a Bee!"

EDWARD LEAR (1812 – 88)

ANTS

in the salt shaker. Ants
in the rice. Floating in
milky cooker water,
crawling out of cups.
Ants scramble up
the walls. They
skitter out of
sight, otherwise
march single file across
the sink, linoleum kitchen
floor. From territory
to territory crumb-
carriers travel like freight.
Oh, pioneers, soldiering
loads against the trails
for their bloated
queen. In an eye-
blink ants turn
into dirt, specks,
into seeds. Seeds
into ants. Crust the
toothpaste tube, added
crunch to the food.
Slip into airtight
plastics, coffee

swimming pools.
Multiple, plural, never
one, scatter laborer,
dancing in paradise.
This here's sugar
country, after all, fire
up the fields, fragrant
smokes somersaulting.
Quick burn, hacked
cane in this tall
sweetgrass region,
whereabout place of
peanut butter sold
in jars, lids electrical
taped, sealing in
their secrets.

JOSEPH O. LEGASPI (1971–)

STILL LIFE

In the fruit
on gran's bedside table,
under the translucent skin
of a grape,
the black pips
at the core
seem to be crawling.

What's going on
inside the greenlit gum
of its flesh
are six ants:
the whiskers
of their legs,
their small
plectrum heads
and snipping mouths.

Soon all the fruit bowl
will be moving.
Already
an apple's breast
has a visible pulse.
A once-dense peach
is deflating.

And what can she do
but stare
from her hospital bed;
seeming all the stiller
for her slow
pink eyelids,
those quick
teaspoon
breaths.

MARK PAJAK (1987–)

A COUPLE

A bee rolls in the yellow rose.
Does she invite his hairy rub?
He scrubs himself in her creamy folds. . . .
When he's done his honey-thieving
at her matrix, whirs free, leaving,
she closes, still tall, chill,
unrumpled on her stem.

BEEHIVE

Within this black hive to-night
There swarm a million bees;
Bees passing in and out the moon,
Bees escaping out the moon,
Bees returning through the moon,
Silver bees intently buzzing,
Silver honey dripping from the swarm of bees
Earth is a waxen cell of the world comb,
And I, a drone,
Lying on my back,
Lipping honey,
Getting drunk with silver honey,
Wish that I might fly out past the moon
And curl forever in some far-off farmyard flower.

JEAN TOOMER (1894–1967)

EROS AND THE BEE
(*After Theocritus*)

A bee, within a rosebud lying,
'Scap'd the infant Love's espying;
With finger stung and sobbing cry,
To his fond mother did he fly.

"Mother," he said, "I faint, I die,
This wound a little wingèd snake,
Which rustics call a bee, did make."

But she answer'd, "If the sting
Of bees be such a painful thing,
What think'st thou of their bitter smart,
The hapless victims of thy dart?"

FABLE

O my children, the ant has a boulder in its mouth.
Pale-white ant rushes with a potato chip
that fell yesterday from our table.

I was like that once – moving rapidly –
taking food home, bearing the weight

because an ant is a lever, its body a physics,
the weight of the chip is nothing to it.

O wonders of the world, I am nothing
compared to the work.

ABIGAIL WENDER (1956–)   53

THE FIRST DAYS
Optima dies prima fugit

The first thing I saw in the morning
Was a huge golden bee ploughing
His burly right shoulder into the belly
Of a sleek yellow pear
Low on a bough.
Before he could find that sudden black honey
That squirms around in there
Inside the seed, the tree could not bear any more.
The pear fell to the ground,
With the bee still half alive
Inside its body.
He would have died if I hadn't knelt down
And sliced the pear gently
A little more open.
The bee shuddered, and returned.
Maybe I should have left him alone there,
Drowning in his own delight.
The best days are the first
To flee, sang the lovely
Musician born in this town
So like my own.
I let the bee go
Among the gasworks at the edge of Mantua.

SINGERS

THE CRICKET

I am sad for the cricket,
Sadder for the late
First century B.C. Tibetans
Who tried to get rid of it.

Billions of yellow-black
Herbivorous villains
Devoured the Himalayan Valley,
Now as good as the Dead Sea,

Mowed prodigiously over
The Yangtze, desecrated
The shrine of the Gods
Of Fruition and Harvest.

A cricket can be a friend.
As individuals they're all right.
Before her exile, Yang Kuei Fei
Held one in her palm.

No wonder the Grand Eunuch
Of the Dowager T'zu Hsi said
Unleash it and it will kill;
Cage it, it will sing.

MARILYN CHIN (1955 –)

TO A CATY-DID

In a branch of willow hid
Sings the evening Caty-did:
From the lofty-locust bough
Feeding on a drop of dew,
In her suit of green arrayed
Hear her singing in the shade –
    Caty-did, Caty-did, Caty-did!

While upon a leaf you tread,
Or repose your little head
On your sheet of shadows laid,
All the day you nothing said:
Half the night your cheery tongue
Revelled out its little song, –
    Nothing else but Caty-did.

From your lodging on the leaf
Did you utter joy or grief?
Did you only mean to say,
I have had my summer's day,
And am passing, soon, away
To the grave of Caty-did:
    Poor, unhappy Caty-did!

But you would have uttered more
Had you known of nature's power;
From the world when you retreat,
And a leaf's your winding sheet,
Long before your spirit fled,
Who can tell but nature said, —
Live again, my Caty-did!
Live, and chatter Caty-did.

Tell me, what did Caty do?
Did she mean to trouble you?
Why was Caty not forbid
To trouble little Caty-did?
Wrong, indeed, at you to fling,
Hurting no one while you sing, —
Caty-did! Caty-did! Caty-did!

Why continue to complain?
Caty tells me she again
Will not give you plague or pain;
Caty says you may be hid,
Caty will not go to bed
While you sing us Caty-did, —
Caty-did! Caty-did! Caty-did!

But, while singing, you forgot
To tell us what did Caty *not:*
Caty did not think of cold,
Flocks retiring to the fold,
Winter with his wrinkles old;
Winter, that yourself foretold
    When you gave us Caty-did.

Stay serenely on your nest;
Caty now will do her best,
All she can, to make you blest;
But you want no human aid, —
Nature, when she formed you, said,
    "Independent you are made,
My dear little Caty-did:
Soon yourself must disappear
With the verdure of the year,"
And to go, we know not where,
    With your song of Caty-did.

CICADAS

The palo verde in the yard comes alive again,
spilling every secret I whispered in my mother's ear:
how I had a crush on the blonde boy in overalls;
how I stole a deck of cards from Zody's but never
used them. The chimpanzee on each card judging me
with eyes that refused to blink. I told my mother this
and many other things though she wasn't really there
but buried in an old cemetery a country away, where
the spirits flew in each November on the orange wings
of monarchs. Since we had no butterfly migration
in Southern California, cicadas would do, their song
not a song exactly, but a scream at the sun, the heat,
the bright yellow flowers of the palo verde – at all
    summer
fires that reminded us that life must go on despite
my grief. *Tell everyone about me!* I yelled at the tree
as I rummaged through the branches for exoskeletons.
The cicadas could never be caught. But I punished them
for their brief lives by crushing the evidence of their
existence between my angry forefinger and sad thumb.

RIGOBERTO GONZÁLEZ (1970 –)

TO AN INSECT

I love to hear thine earnest voice,
    Wherever thou art hid,
Thou testy little dogmatist,
    Thou pretty Katydid!
Thou mindest me of gentlefolks, –
    Old gentlefolks are they, –
Thou say'st an undisputed thing
    In such a solemn way.

Thou art a female, Katydid!
    I know it by the trill
That quivers through thy piercing notes,
    So petulant and shrill.
I think there is a knot of you
    Beneath the hollow tree, –
A knot of spinster Katydids, –
    Do Katydids drink tea?

O, tell me where did Katy live,
    And what did Katy do?
And was she very fair and young,
    And yet so wicked too?
Did Katy love a naughty man,
    Or kiss more cheeks than one?
I warrant Kitty did no more
    Than many a Kate has done.

OLIVER WENDELL HOLMES (1809–94)

TO THE GRASSHOPPER
AND THE CRICKET

Green little vaulter in the sunny grass,
 Catching your heart up at the feel of June,
 Sole voice that's heard amidst the lazy noon,
When ev'n the bees lag at the summoning brass; –
And you, warm little housekeeper, who class
 With those who think the candles come too soon,
 Loving the fire, and with your tricksome tune
Nick the glad silent moments as they pass; –

Oh sweet and tiny cousins, that belong,
 One to the fields, the other to the hearth,
Both have your sunshine; both, though small,
  are strong
 At your clear hearts; and both were sent on earth
To sing in thoughtful ears this natural song –
 In doors and out, – summer and winter, – Mirth.

LEIGH HUNT (1784–1859)

HAIKU

I beseech thee,
Chant a prayer,
Summer cicadas.

Summer cicadas:
They cry
Even while making love.

Ah, the cicadas cry!
As though to turn my house
To stone.

ON THE GRASSHOPPER AND CRICKET

The Poetry of earth is never dead:
    When all the birds are faint with the hot sun,
    And hide in cooling trees, a voice will run
From hedge to hedge about the new-mown mead;
That is the Grasshopper's – he takes the lead
    In summer luxury, – he has never done
    With his delights; for when tired out with fun
He rests at ease beneath some pleasant weed.
The poetry of earth is ceasing never:
    On a lone winter evening, when the frost
        Has wrought a silence, from the stove there
            shrills
The Cricket's song, in warmth increasing ever,
    And seems to one in drowsiness half lost,
        The Grasshopper's among some grassy hills.

JOHN KEATS (1795–1821)

THEIR CAPS BLOWN OFF,

dandelion floss drift in the wind,
and are caught in little cloud puffs
on my window screen in Shimogyo-ku.
At first, I thought they were insects
and looked closely at them for legs.

The summer threatens to go on,
but the staccato *shichishichishichi*,
from the tymbals of buzzing cicadas
will all but cease. I don't know
when the quiet happened,
though I'm always aware
of the sounds of crying.

At the Eikando Temple
where the Buddha looks back at me,
to hurry, come along,
the maple leaves are changing
color around the edges,
the singing insects leaving summer.

All the signs of autumn are here,
my knees cracking,
arthritic fingers swelling.

Like a cat in the susuki grass,
waiting to leap at the late
birds and insects of summer,
the cold waits,
everything struggling to turn,
knowing that the insect calls
would return
and rise the following spring.

JULIET S. KONO (1943–)

CRICKETS ON A STRIKE

The foolish queen of fairyland
From her milk-white throne in a lily-bell,
Gave command to her cricket-band
To play for her when the dew-drops fell.

But the cold dew spoiled their instruments
And they play for the foolish queen no more.
Instead those sturdy malcontents
Play sharps and flats in my kitchen floor.

TO THE CICADA

Cicada, drunk with drops of dew,
What musician equals you
In the rural solitude?
On your perch within the wood,
Scraping to your heart's desire
Dusky sides with notchy feet,
Thrilling, shrilling, fast and sweet,
Like the music of a lyre.
Dear Cicada, I entreat,
Sing the wood-nymphs something new,
So that from his arboured seat
Pan himself may answer you,
Till every inmost glade rejoices
With your loud alternate voices.
And I may listen, and forget
All the thorns, the doubts and fears,
Love in this sad heart hath set —
Listen, and forget them all;
And so, with music in mine ears,
Where the plane-tree-shadows steep
The ground with coolness, softly fall
Into a noontide sleep.

MELEAGER (1st Century BCE)
TRANSLATED BY WILLIAM ALLINGHAM

ODES OF ANACREON: ODE XXXIV

Oh thou, of all creation blest,
Sweet insect that delight'st in rest
Upon the wild wood's leafy tops,
To drink the dew that morning drops,
And chirp thy song with such a glee,
That happiest kings many envy thee,

Whatever decks the velvet field,
What'er the circling seasons yield,
Whatever buds, whatever blows,
For thee it buds, for thee it grows.
Nor yet art thou the peasant's fear,
To him thy friendly notes are dear;
For thou art mild as matin dew;
And still, when summer's flowery hue
Begins to paint the bloomy plain,
We hear thy sweet prophetic strain;
Thy sweet prophetic strain we hear,
And bless the notes and thee revere!
The Muses love thy shrilly tone;
Apollo calls thee all his own;
'Twas he who gave that voice to thee,
'Tis he who tunes thy minstrelsy.

Unworn by age's dim decline,
The fadeless blooms of youth are thine.
Melodious insect, child of earth,
In wisdom mirthful, wise in mirth;
Exempt from every weak decay,
That withers vulgar frames away,
With not a drop of blood to stain
The current of thy purer vein;
So blest an age is past by thee,
Thou seem'st – a little deity!

THOMAS MOORE (1779–1852)

CRICKET CRICKET

When I am alone on a summer night, and
there is a cricket in the house, I always feel
that things could be worse. Maybe it is raining,
and then thunder and lightning are shaking the
house. The power goes out, and I must grope
around in the darkness for a candle. At last,
the candle is found, but where are the matches?
I always keep them in that drawer. I knock over
a vase, but it doesn't break. Afraid of what
I might break, I return to my chair and sit
there in the darkness. The lightning is striking
all around the house. Then I remember the cricket,
and I listen for its chirping. Soon, the storm
passes, and the lights come back on. An eerie
green silence fills my home. I am worried that
the cricket may have been struck by some light-
ning of its own.

FOREBODING

Cricket, why wilt thou crush me with thy cry?
How can such light sound weigh so heavily!
Behold the grass is sere, the cold dews fall,
The world grows empty – yes, I know it all,
                The knell of joy I hear.

Oh, long ago the swallows hence have flown,
And sadly sings the sea in undertone;
The wild vine crimsons o'er the rough gray stone;
The stars of winter rise, the cool winds moan;
                Fast wanes the golden year.

O cricket, cease thy sorrowful refrain
This summer's glory comes not back again,
But others wait with flowers and sun and rain;
Why wakest thou this haunting sense of pain,
                Of loss, regret, and fear?

Clear sounds thy note above the waves' low sigh,
Clear through the breathing wind that wanders by,
Clear through the rustle of dry grasses tall;
Thou chantest, "Joy is dead!"   I know it all,
                The winter's woe is near.

CELIA THAXTER (1835 – 94)

CICADAS

You know those windless summer evenings, swollen
    to stasis
by too-substantial melodies, rich as a
running-down record, ground round
to full quiet. Even the leaves
have thick tongues.

And if the first crickets quicken then,
other inhabitants, at window or door
or rising from table, feel in the lungs
a slim false-freshness, by this
trick of the ear.

Chanters of miracles took for a simple sign
the Latin cicada, because of his long waiting
and sweet change in daylight, and his singing
all his life, pinched on the ash leaf,
heedless of ants.

Others made morals; all were puzzled and joyed
by this gratuitous song. Such a plain thing
morals could not surround, nor listening:
not "chirr" nor "cri-cri." There is no straight
way of approaching it.

This thin uncomprehended song it is
springs healing questions into binding air.
Fabre, by firing all the municipal cannon
under a piping tree, found out
cicadas cannot hear.

RICHARD WILBUR (1921–2017)

SPARKLERS AND SWOOPERS

BLUE GHOST FIREFLY
Phausis reticulata

The female is small
and larviform,
like a grimy rice grain.

Up close you see
her reticulated,
transparent back,

its epaulettes of light.
Sweet love
coiled round your eggs,

like a diminutive dragon
guarding your hoard,
its wet, nested glow.

It's the rest
of your life's work
to make yourself a lid,

a shield, a reinforced roof.
I too keep guard –
my daughters

the softest part of me —
and will die
at my post.

THE DRAGONFLY

You are made of almost nothing
But of enough
To be great eyes
And diaphanous double vans;
To be ceaseless movement,
Unending hunger
Grappling love.

Link between water and air,
Earth repels you.
Light touches you only to shift into iridescence
Upon your body and wings.

Twice-born, predator,
You split into the heat.
Swift beyond calculation or capture
You dart into the shadow
Which consumes you.

You rocket into the day.
But at last, when the wind flattens the grasses,
For you, the design and purpose stop.

And you fall
With the other husks of summer.

LOUISE BOGAN (1897–1970)   81

CHANT TO THE FIRE-FLY

Wau wau tay see!
Wau wau tay see!
E mow e shin
Tshe bwau ne baun-e wee!
Be eghaun – be eghaun – ewee!
Wa wau tay see!
Wa wau tay see!
Was sa koon ain je gun
Was sa koon ain je gun.

Fire-fly, fire-fly! bright little thing,
Light me to bed, and my song I will sing.
Give me your light, as you fly o'er my head,
That I may merrily go to my bed.
Give me your light o'er the grass as you creep,
That I may joyfully go to my sleep.
Come little fire-fly – come little beast –
Come! and I'll make you to-morrow a feast.
Come little candle that flies as I sing,
Bright little fairy-bug – night's little king;
Come, and I'll dance as you guide me along,
Come, and I'll pay you, my bug, with a song.

82   OJIBWE (*c.* 1848)
TRANSLATED BY HENRY R. SCHOOLCRAFT
(1793–1864)

THE DRAGONFLY

Now, when my roses are half buds, half flowers,
  And loveliest, the king of flies has come –
It was a fleeting visit, all too brief;
  In three short minutes he had seen them all,
And rested, too, upon an apple leaf.

There, his round shoulders humped with emeralds,
  A gorgeous opal crown set on his head,
And all those shining honours to his breast –
  "My garden is a lovely place," thought I,
"But is it worthy of so fine a guest?"

He rested there, upon that apple leaf –
  "See, see," I cried amazed, "his opal crown,
And all those emeralds clustered round his head!"
  "His breast, my dear, how lovely was his breast" –
The voice of my Belovèd quickly said.

"See, see his gorgeous crown, that shines
  With all those jewels bulging round its rim" –
I cried aloud at night, in broken rest.
  Back came the answer quickly, in my dream –
"His breast, my dear, how lovely was his breast!"

W. H. DAVIES (1871–1940)

THE DRAGONFLY

When to avoid chill winter's snow
   The gilded insect takes its flight,
Too often bramble, bush or brier,
   Has torn its wings so frail and bright.

So youth with all its strength and fire,
   Sipping the sweets on every side,
Receives a fatal wound from thorns
   Which the gay flowers of pleasure hide.

THE DRAGONFLY

Fallen, so freshly fallen
From his estates of air,
He made on the gritty path
A five-inch funeral car,
New Hampshire's lesser dragon
In the grip of his kidnapers.
A triumph of *chinoiserie*
He seemed, in green and gold
Enameling, pin-brained,
With swizzle-stick for tail,
The breastplate gemmed between.
What a gallantry of pomp
In that royal spread of wings! —
Four leaves of thinnest mica,
Or, better, of the skin
Of water, if water had a skin.
Semaphores, at rest,
Of the frozen invisible,
They caught a glinting light
In the hairlines of their scripture
When a vagrom current stirred
And made them feign to flutter.
It was a slow progress,
A thing of fits and starts,
With bands of black attendants

Tugging at the wings
And under the crested feelers
At the loose-hinged head
(So many eyes he had, which were
The eyes?), still others pushing
From behind, where a pair
Of ornamental silks
That steered him in his flights
Gave tenuous pincer-hold.
Admire, I said to myself,
How he lords it over them,
Grounded though he may be
After his blue-sky transports;
But see how they honor him,
His servants at the feast,
In a passion of obsequies,
With chomping mandibles
And wildly waving forelegs
Telegraphing news abroad
Of their booty's worth; oh praise this
Consummate purity
Of the bestriding will!
In a scaled-down mythology
These myrmidons could stand
For the separate atoms of St. George
(Why not?). And fancy drove
Me on, my science kneeling

Before such witless tools,
To pay my tithe of awe
And read the resurrection-sign
In the motion of the death.
But then I saw,
When an imperceptible gust
Abruptly hoisted sails
And flipped my hero over . . .
In the reversal of the scene
I saw the sixfold spasm
Of his tucked-in claws,
The cry of writhing nerve-ends,
And down his membrane-length
A tide of gray pulsation.
I wheeled. The scorpion sun,
Stoking its belly-fires,
Exploded overhead, and the rain
Came down: scales, tortuous wires,
Flakings of green and gold.

STANLEY KUNITZ (1905 – 2006)

BLEACH

I mistook their eggs for mosquito larvae,
breeding in cool silence below stagnant water,

not those graceful, otherworldly creatures
born as summer's green gold tips into fall.

One more week they would have flown,
buzzing the reeds with gauzy, biplanar wings –

suspended like held breath in a sea of air,
or perched on the whipcrack of a branch

as the world goes still, a gift you never
asked for, as if your heart's wound

could be healed by their filigreed perfection.
Instead, these endless dragonflies, seared, surfacing in

the rain barrel, curled into dead interrogative –
risen from the murky swell into which I'd poured.

FIREFLIES IN THE CORN
SHE SPEAKS

Look at the little darlings in the corn!
   The rye is taller than you, who think yourself
So high and mighty: look how the heads are borne
   Dark and proud on the sky, like a number of
      knights
Passing with spears and pennants and manly scorn.

Knights indeed! – much knight I know will ride
   With his head held high-serene against the sky!
Limping and following rather at my side
   Moaning for me to love him! – O darling rye
How I adore you for your simple pride!

And the dear, dear fireflies wafting in between
   And over the swaying corn-stalks, just above
All the dark-feathered helmets, like little green
   Stars come low and wandering here for love
Of these dark knights, shedding their delicate sheen!

I thank you I do, you happy creatures, you dears,
   Riding the air, and carrying all the time
Your little lanterns behind you! Ah, it cheers
   My soul to see you settling and trying to climb
The corn-stalks, tipping with fire the spears.

All over the dim corn's motion, against the blue
   Dark sky of night, a wandering glitter, a swarm
Of questing brilliant souls going out with their true
   Proud knights to battle! Sweet, how I warm
My poor, my perished soul with the sight of you!

THE MOWER TO THE GLOW-WORMS

Ye living lamps, by whose dear light
The nightingale does sit so late,
And studying all the summer night,
Her matchless songs does meditate;

Ye country comets, that portend
No war nor prince's funeral,
Shining unto no higher end
Than to presage the grass's fall;

Ye glow-worms, whose officious flame
To wand'ring mowers shows the way,
That in the night have lost their aim,
And after foolish fires do stray;

Your courteous lights in vain you waste,
Since Juliana here is come,
For she my mind hath so displac'd
That I shall never find my home.

ANDREW MARVELL (1621–78)

THE DRAGONFLY

Under the pond, among rocks
Or in the bramble of the water wood,
He is at home, and feeds the small
Remorseless craving of his dream,

His cruel delight; until in May
The dream transforms him with itself
And from his depths he rises out,
An exile from the brutal night.

He rises out, the aged one
Imprisoned in the dying child,
And spreads his wings to the new sun:
Climbing, he withers into light.

FIREFLIES

The lights come on and stay on under the trees.
Visibly a whole neighbourhood inhabits the dusk,
so punctual and in place it seems to deny
dark its dominion. Nothing will go astray,
the porch lamps promise. Sudden, as though a match
failed to ignite at the foot of the garden, the first
    squibs
trouble the eye. Impossible not to share
that sportive, abortive, clumsy, where-are-we-now
dalliance with night, such soothing restlessness.
What should we make of fireflies, their quick flare
of promise and disappointment, their throwaway
    style?
Our heads turn this way and that. We are loath to
    miss
such jauntiness in nature. Those fugitive selves,
winged and at random! Our flickery might-have-beens
come up from the woods to haunt us! Our yet-to-be
as tentative frolic! What do the fireflies say?
That loneliness made light of becomes at last
convivial singleness? That any antic spark
cruising the void might titillate creation?
And whether they spend themselves, or go to ground,
or drift with their lights out, they have left the gloom,
for as long as our eyes take to absorb such absence,

less than it seemed, as childless and deprived
as Chaos and Old Night. But ruffled too,
as though it unearthed some memory of light
from its long blackout, a hospitable core
fit home for fireflies, brushed by fireflies' wings.

DRAGONFLIES IN LOVE

They piggyback in parabolas
of lust, looping through noonbright air,
writing their gene-scripted history
over and over as elegantly
as the hushed wing fluttering
with which an eagle, no more than ten
or twelve yards away, brakes,
before talon-spearing a rainbow trout
that caught fatal sunlight.

Unabashed, as if boasting of
needle quick, nuanced motion,
they knife the air, slice blue light
into shreds of silver
drifting across Oak Pond.
The splash of a frog, slither of a snake
do little to distract from
the aura of dragonflies in love.

A hint of breeze wrinkles the sheen
of silver water, as if suggesting
the great age for which this ritual
aerial merge has gone on.
Bodies of blue, green, black, orange,
wings as gossamer blurry as light,

they dart in diaphanous swerves of longing,
the pulse by which heat shimmers and dances
pounding through their thin bright veins.

WATCHING FIREFLIES

Fireflies from the Enchanted Mountains
come through the screen this autumn night
and settle on my shirt

my lute and my books grow cold

outside, above the eaves
they are hard to tell from the stars

they sail over the well
each reflecting a mate

in the garden they pass chrysanthemums
flares of color against the dark

white-haired and sad
I try to read their code
wanting a prediction:
will I be here next year
to watch them?

TU FU (712–70)
TRANSLATED BY DAVID YOUNG

GLIDERS

GLIDERS

THE BUTTERFLY

The Butterfly the ancient Grecians made
The soul's fair emblem, and its only name –
But of the soul, escaped the slavish trade
Of earthly life! – For in this mortal frame
Ours is the reptile's lot, much toil, much blame,
Manifold motions making little speed,
And to deform and kill the things whereon we feed.

SAMUEL TAYLOR COLERIDGE (1772–1834)

SEASON OF THE BUTTERFLIES

The world around me is wildflower teeming,
small yellow, round orange petal, the lavender
and the sun coming from earth,
even the webs of finery shining in light
and it takes just a sheer brief atmosphere
flying inches above this beloved earth
with the many thousand wings, all colors,
truly the Cíbola other men saw.
The entire sky moved in those days,
shining like valuable elements with mineral longing.

Once these were chrysalis, worm, the many-legged,
each holding their part of the god
of butterflies, chrysalis opened at the back.
Without teeth some ate their way through the silken
        shroud of life
or made long other journeys
to fly above this illumined world.

Even if I could live that way one day,
if only, in the illuminated world of another code,
step out of my body of silk flesh
open out of the pain clothing
where I live so mortally beautiful, a soul of light,
even then I would never be so rich, so perfect

as the winged lives moving
flower to flower,
pollen to pollen,
immortal to the spirit of mortal memory
that can't relinquish its hold
on this life stem.

"ALL AS THAT MOTH"

All as that moth call'd Underwing, alighted,
Pacing and turning, so by slips discloses
Her sober simple coverlid underplighted
To colour as smooth and fresh as cheeks of roses,
{ Her showy leaves staid watchet counterfoiling
{ Her showy leaves with gentle watchet foiling
Even so my thought the rose and grey disposes

MOTH

Pressed up against the narrow pane, the moth is rust,
its wings the colour of blood drying on stone.

The house and sky are one cubic dark, through whose
    thin walls
the boy moves like a silken cloth,

buffing the brass urns and pewter mugs he touches.
Clots of light, straining through his palms, float in
    the air.

Dawn is a mile off, but when the house gets there,
a hard edge of fire cuts through the glass

and through the night's restraint: the boy grabs at the
    moth
and stumbles. His prize is just a shock

of sulphur wings that thrash in his hands and vaporize
while he falls headlong, his hands flecked with pollen-
    dust.

He comes to the window again, next dawn. There is
    no moth
to reach for. He slashes his palms on the fire-
    sharpened glass.

RANJIT HOSKOTE (1969–)

LITTLE OFFER

For their kind, not a moment's doubt.
Unwavering devotees,
they never hesitate for lack
of ideology.

I know I'm neither first nor last
of my kind to admire
the way they aim at radiance
and take for their last pyre

the first open flame. A shadow
in shadows at their rite,
I am, as always, paid no mind,
as I illuminate

nothing. The wordless watchword must
closer, closer hum
from the heavy place in their weightless
bodies, the tripped alarm

silenced only as the scales fall
singed from their whole selves.
I'll wipe, again, their dust and ash
en masse from sills and shelves.

Misguided still means guided somewhere,
still *means*. Great Light,
I'll trade you all my lofty thoughts
(never aloft) and bright

ideas (always unlit) and credos,
edicts, theorems, tired
metaphors of moths-to-flames
for my pair of wings on fire.

THE NIGHT MOTHS

Out of the night to my leafy porch they came,
   A thousand moths. Did He who made the toad
   Give them their wings upon the starry road?
Restless and wild they circle round the flame,
Frail wonder-shapes that man can never tame –
   Whirl like the blown flakes of December snows,
   Tinted with amber, violet and rose,
Markt with hieroglyphs that have no name.

Out of the summer darkness pours the flight:
   Unknown the wild processional they keep.
What lures them to this rush of mad delight?
   Why are they called from nothingness and sleep?
Why this rich beauty wandering the night?
   Do they go lost and aimless to the deep?

MONARCHS

All morning, as I sit thinking of you,
the Monarchs are passing. Seven stories up,
to the left of the river, they are making their way
south, their wings the dark red of
your hands like butchers' hands, the raised
veins of their wings like your scars.
I could scarcely feel your massive rough
palms on me, your touch was so light,
the delicate chapped scrape of an insect's leg
across my breast. No one had ever
touched me before. I didn't know enough to
open my legs, but felt your thighs,
feathered with red-gold hairs,
                    opening
between my legs like a
pair of wings.
The hinged print of my blood on your thigh –
a winged creature pinned there –
and then you left, as you were to leave
over and over, the butterflies moving
in masses past my window, floating
south to their transformation, crossing over
borders in the night, the diffuse blood-red
cloud of them, my body under yours,
the beauty and silence of the great migrations.

SHARON OLDS (1942 –)   109

GREAT MOTH COMES FROM HIS PAPERY CAGE

Gone is the worm, that tunnel body. Gone is the
        mouth that loved leaves and tomatoes.
Gone are the innumerable feet.

He is beautiful now, and shivers into the air
as if he has always known how,
who crawled and crawled, all summer.
He has wide wings, with a flare at the bottom.
The moon excites him. The heat of the night
        excites him.

But, where did the dance come from?
Surely not out of a simple winter's sleep.
Surely it's more than ambition, this new architecture!
What could it be, that does it?

Let me look closer, and a long time, the next time
I see green-blooded worm crawling and curling
hot day after hot day
among the leaves and the smooth, proud tomatoes.

LUNA MOTH

No eye that sees could fail to remark you:
like any leaf the rain leaves fixed to and
flat against the barn's gray shingle. But

what leaf, this time of year, is so pale,
the pale of leaves when they've lost just
enough green to become the green that *means*

loss and more loss, approaching? Give up
the flesh enough times, and whatever is lost
gets forgotten: that was the thought that I

woke to, those words in my head. I rose,
I did not dress, I left no particular body
sleeping and, stepping into the hour, I saw

you, strange sign, at once transparent and
impossible to entirely see through, and how
still: the still of being unmoved, and then

the still of no longer being able to be
moved. If I think of a heart, his, as I've
found it. . . . If I think of, increasingly, my

own. . . . If I look at you now, as from above,
and see the diva when she is caught in mid-
triumph, arms half-raised, the body as if

set at last free of the green sheath that has –
how many nights? – held her, it is not
without remembering another I once saw:

like you, except that something, a bird, some
wild and necessary hunger, had gotten to it;
and like the diva, but now broken, splayed

and torn, the green torn piecemeal from her.
I remember the hands, and – how small they
seemed, bringing the small ripped thing to me.

WHITE BUTTERFLIES

I

Clematis paniculata sweetens one side of Howard
    Street.
White butterflies in pairs flutter over the white
    flowers.
In white kimonos, giggling and whispering,
The butterflies titter and flutter their silk fans,
End-of-summer cabbage butterflies, in white pairs.
Sweet autumn clematis feeds these delicate souls
    perfume.
I remember how we met, how shyly.

II

Four months of drought on the East End ends.
Ten thousand windshield wipers wiping the tears
    away.
The back roads are black.
The ocean runs around barking under the delicious
    rain, so happy.
Traditional household cleaners polish the imperial
    palace floors
Of heaven spotless. THUNDER. Cleanliness and
    order
Bring universal freshness and good sense to the
    Empire. LIGHTNING.

III

I have never had a serious thought in my life on
    Gibson Lane.
A man turning into cremains is standing on the
    beach.
I used to walk my dog along the beach.
This afternoon I had to put him down.
Jimmy my boy, my sweetyboy, my Jimmy.
It is night, and outside the house, at eleven o'clock,
The lawn sprinklers come on in the rain.

A LUNA MOTH
For Elizabeth Bishop

For six days and nights
a luna moth, pale green,
pinned herself to the sliding screen —
a prize specimen in a lepidopterist's dream.

Tuesday's wind knocked her off the deck.
She tacked herself back up again.
During Wednesday's rain she disappeared
and reappeared on Thursday
to meditate and sun herself,
recharging her dreams from dawn to dusk,
and all night draining the current from
the deck's electric lantern.

A kimono just wider than my hand,
her two pairs of flattened wings were pale
gray-green panels of the sheerest crêpe de Chine.
Embroidered on each sleeve, a drowsing eye
appeared to watch the pair of eyes
on the wings below quite wide awake.
But they're *all* fake.
Nature's *trompe l'oeil* gives the luna
eyes of a creature twice her size.

The head was covered with snow-white fur.
Once, I got so close
it rippled when I breathed on her.
She held herself so still,
she looked dead. I stroked
the hem of her long, sweeping tail;
her wings dosed my fingers with a green-gold dust.
I touched her feathery antennae.
She twitched and calmly
reattached herself a quarter inch west,
tuning into the valley miles away
a moment-by-moment weather report
broadcast by a compatriot,
catching the scent of a purely
sexual call; hearing sounds
I never hear, having
the more primitive ear.

Serene
in the middle of the screen,
she ruled the grid of her domain
oblivious to her collected kin –
the homely brown varieties of moth
tranced-out and immobile,
or madly fanning their paper wings,
bashing their brains out on the bulb.
Surrounded by her dull-witted cousins,

she is herself a sort of bulb,
and Beauty is a kind of brilliance,
burning self-absorbed, giving little,
indifferent as a reflecting moon.

Clinging to the screen despite my comings
and goings, she never seemed to mind the ride.
At night, when I slid the glass door shut,
I liked to think I introduced her
to her perfect match
hatched from an illusion –
like something out of the Brothers Grimm –
who, mirroring her dreamy stillness,
pining for a long-lost twin,
regarded her exactly as she regarded him.

This morning,
a weekend guest sunbathing on the deck,
sun-blind, thought the wind had blown
a five-dollar bill against the screen.
He grabbed the luna, gasped,
and flung her to the ground.
She lay a long moment in the grass,
then fluttered slowly to the edge of the woods
where, sometimes at dawn,
deer nibble the wild raspberry bushes.

JANE SHORE (1947–)

CORONAL

Arched, a tawny
Fritillary pivots on petals,
butterfly wings closed as she

turns. I understand
shutting tight: nothing revealed
except the received,

silence handed down,
even absence. Coiled tight,
the proboscis unfurls

to suck deep of pistils,
a wild bittersweet within a center
becoming harder to locate.

More like a stutter as she hops
to another bloom, as if *never*
and *always* merge but will

not hold. Can not last. Morphosis
shimmering like the Queen's
diadem, just out of reach.

TO A BUTTERFLY

I've watched you now a full half-hour,
Self-poised upon that yellow flower;
And, little Butterfly! indeed
I know not if you sleep or feed.
How motionless! – not frozen seas
More motionless! and then
What joy awaits you, when the breeze
Hath found you out among the trees,
And calls you forth again!

This plot of Orchard-ground is ours;
My trees they are, my Sister's flowers;
Here rest your wings when they are weary,
Here lodge as in a sanctuary!
Come often to us, fear no wrong;
Sit near us on the bough!
We'll talk of sunshine and of song;
And summer days when we were young;
Sweet childish days, that were as long
As twenty days are now.

LEAPERS

r-p-o-p-h-e-s-s-a-g-r

                    r-p-o-p-h-e-s-s-a-g-r
                    who
a)s w(e loo)k
upnowgath
        PPEGORHRASS
                              eringint(o-
aThe):l
     eA
       !p:
S   a
              (r
rIvInG   .gRrEaPsPhOs)
                            to
rea(be)rran(com)gi(e)ngly
,grasshopper;

E. E. CUMMINGS (1894–1962)

MANTIS

She stills herself,
a green meditation,
angled with desire
for aphid, moth.

Icon, on guard,
she is threat posed
as prophet. A body
of tricks, mischief

made leaf, flowering
to thorn; a small
violence. Trauma
is feast.

Mantis, wild queen,
her face is geometry
at play; a compass
for the dead.

RECKLESS SONNET
#2

How lavish are the pheromones? How iridescent
the light if there is light
radiating from the body,
for the compound eyes that cannot afford mistaking
stem for leg, leaf for wing?
How stunning is *heat* in such a coupling
even or especially for the praying mantis
whose female eats the male after that single fuck?
And how does one turn to sleep
in the same bed once made bloody
first with love then with love –
how does one stay
seated in the kitchen listening to the percolator
after that knowledge?

KIMIKO HAHN (1955 –)

THE SEVENTEEN-YEAR LOCUST

There in its tiny tomb of D
NA, held in the mute loam
It is made of, earthbound
& antediluvian, each nymph

Busies itself sucking sap
From a tree root. True
As twelve solid-gold watches,
When the time comes, the locust

Tunnels open a chimney
Of light – a mere eyehole
Of dust & sap that hardens
Into mortar. On the brink

It waits for green to draw out
God's praise & lamentation.
As if a new bead for a rattle,
It clings to bark & eats itself empty.

THE GRASSHOPPER
To My Noble Friend, Mr. Charles Cotton

O thou that swing'st upon the waving hair
    Of some well-fillèd oaten beard,
Drunk every night with a delicious tear
    Dropped thee from heaven, where now th' art reared;

The joys of earth and air are thine entire,
    That with thy feet and wings dost hop and fly;
And, when thy poppy works, thou dost retire
    To thy carved acorn-bed to lie.

Up with the day, the sun thou welcom'st then,
    Sport'st in the gilt-plats of his beams,
And all these merry days mak'st merry men,
    Thyself, and melancholy streams.

But ah, the sickle! Golden ears are cropped;
    Ceres and Bacchus bid good night;
Sharp, frosty fingers all your flowers have topped,
    And what scythes spared, winds shave off quite.

Poor verdant fool, and now green ice! thy joys,
    Large and as lasting as thy perch of grass,
Bid us lay in 'gainst winter rain, and poise
    Their floods with an o'erflowing glass.

Thou best of men and friends! we will create
  A genuine summer in each other's breast,
And spite of this cold time and frozen fate,
  Thaw us a warm seat to our rest.

Our sacred hearths shall burn eternally,
  As vestal flames; the North Wind, he
Shall strike his frost-stretched wings, dissolve, and fly
  This Etna in epitome.

Dropping December shall come weeping in,
  Bewail th'usurping of his reign:
But when in showers of old Greek we begin,
  Shall cry he hath his crown again!

Night, as clear Hesper, shall our tapers whip
  From the light casements where we play,
And the dark hag from her black mantle strip,
  And stick there everlasting day.

Thus richer than untempted kings are we,
  That, asking nothing, nothing need:
Though lords of all what seas embrace, yet he
  That wants himself is poor indeed.

THE LOCUSTS

The plain dries outward from its heart.
The wise flat-bottomed clouds depart
With all their secrets. Green and gold
The land still tries to look controlled
But one leaf panics. It will start

Now. A chirring numbs the air.
Live shrouds abruptly from nowhere
Fill up the failing streams like dirt.
Each tree puts on a dull brown shirt
And slumps, bowed down with care.

You think first: This is no rain
Of locusts, rather my own brain
At work, whose preconceptions dye
The whole world drab. Or bluntly: I
Am dreaming, or insane.

The next day dawns upon no dream.
There is wide evidence of Them,
Such as the myriad dead or maimed
In furrows, in that yet unnamed
Trickle of corpses, once a stream.

Step gingerly; for they were real,
The locusts, after all.
Wearing opaque goggles (proof
Of a vestigial inner life?)
They have the dead hue of the useful,

The weak husk of no great event.
You feel nothing. It is time you went
Back to where everything was clear,
Where trouble was a limpid source to peer
Deep into, heaven-sent

Mirrorscope, green, wet,
All echo, orchid, and egret
In pure transports recalling you.
Go. A young man before you do
Is apt to roll a cigarette

And talk. Come spring (he says)
The grubs will hatch from crevices
To eat up anything that may have bloomed.
How strange, with all of it foredoomed,
His caring for that scant green is!

What can be said to him? The glue
Of dead wings thickens on your shoe.
Indeed, only when far behind
Does the experience make a kind
Of weird sense. One night over the bayou

Certain great clouds you have seen before
Move in, give way to a downpour.
They have been told at last, it seems,
About the flayed trees and the choked streams.
Rain wakes you, pounding on the door.

CRYPTIC MIMICRY

Admit it. You are drawn to beauty,
that false god of line

breaks and white irony.
Why should the orchid mantis hide

among other pink and white petals
and not showcase its anther cap

and labellum, its accented flecks
of cherry and peach to lure prey,

to snatch viceroys and queen
butterflies out of the air –

Tales of Oriental beauty drew
men East and now *Hymenopus coronatus*

decorates American homes.
But look, I am no pet.

My jeans too tight, my button-
down tucked in neatly, but I line

my eyes in rose, I write
in English. Praying in traces

of my heathen tongue, I have come,
to raze all ships sailing for Empire.

RAJIV MOHABIR (1981–)

THE PRAYING MANTIS

From whence arrived the praying mantis?
From outer space, or lost Atlantis?
I glimpse the grim, green metal mug
That masks this pseudo-saintly bug,
Orthopterous, also carnivorous,
And faintly whisper, Lord deliver us.

PRAYING MANTIS

Not quite
Well-rounded,
The praying mantis is
All angles as she
Gangles in shyly
To join in
The party. Her
Filament-thin legs
Are born
Stilts with built-in
Forks to pin down
Her supper, her face
A swaying
Equilateral
Triangle like an
Alien's, her
Panoramic
Quizzical eye
Rolling round for
A suitable partner.
Finding no one
Eligible, she takes
Off on sudden
Wings to land deftly
On a strand of dewy

Green grass where she
Takes cover, waits
Hungrily again
For that delectably
Juicy
Lover.

THE GRASSHOPPER

1

Voice of the summer wind,
Joy of the summer plain,
Life of the summer hours,
Carol clearly, bound along.
No Tithon thou as poets feign
(Shame fall 'em, they are deaf and blind),
But an insect lithe and strong,
Bowing the seeded summer flowers.
Prove their falsehood and thy quarrel,
    Vaulting on thine airy feet.
Clap thy shielded sides and carol,
    Carol clearly, chirrup sweet.
Thou art a mailèd warrior in youth and strength
        complete;
                Armed cap-a-pie
                Full fair to see;
                Unknowing fear,
                Undreading loss,
        A gallant cavalier,
        Sans peur et sans reproche,
        In sunlight and in shadow,
        The Bayard of the meadow.

2

I would dwell with thee,
    Merry grasshopper,
Thou art so glad and free,
    And as light as air;
Thou hast no sorrow or tears,
Thou hast no compt of years,
No withered immortality,
But a short youth sunny and free.
Carol clearly, bound along,
    Soon thy joy is over,
A summer of loud song,
    And slumbers in the clover.
What hast thou to do with evil
In thine hour of love and revel,
    In thy heat of summer pride,
Pushing the thick roots aside
Of the singing flowerèd grasses,
That brush thee with their silken tresses?
What hast thou to do with evil,
Shooting, singing, ever springing
    In and out the emerald glooms,
Ever leaping, ever singing,
    Lighting on the golden blooms?

WEAVERS

ARACHNE

I watch her in the corner there,
As, restless, bold, and unafraid,
She slips and floats along the air
Till all her subtile house is made.

Her home, her bed, her daily food,
All from that hidden store she draws;
She fashions it and knows it good,
By instinct's strong and sacred laws.

No tenuous threads to weave her nest,
She seeks and gathers there or here;
But spins it from her sacred breast,
Renewing still, till leaves are sere.

Then, worn with toil, and tired of life,
In vain her shining traps are set.
Her frost hath hushed the insect strife
And gilded flies her charm forget.

But swinging in the snares she spun,
She sways to every wintry wind;
Her joy, her toil, her errand done,
Her corse the sport of winds unkind.

Poor sister of the spinster clan!
I too from out my store within
My daily life and living plan,
My home, my rest, my pleasure spin.

I know thy heart when heartless hands
Sweep all that hard-earned web away:
Destroy its pearled and glittering bands,
And leave thee homeless by the way.

I know thy peace when all is done,
Each anchored thread, each tiny knot,
Soft shining in the autumn sun;
A sheltered, silent, tranquil lot.

I know what thou hast never known —
Sad presage to a soul allowed —
That not for a life I spin, alone,
But day by day I spin my shroud.

ARACHNE

Twixt devil and deep sea, man hacks his caves;
Birth, death; one, many; what is true, and seems;
Earth's vast hot iron, cold space's empty waves:

King spider, walks the velvet roof of streams:
Must bird and fish, must god and beast avoid:
Dance, like nine angels, on pin-point extremes.

His gleaming bubble between void and void,
Tribe-membrane, that by mutual tension stands,
Earth's surface film, is at a breath destroyed.

Bubbles gleam brightest with least depth of lands
But two is least can with full tension strain,
Two molecules; one, and the film disbands.

We two suffice. But oh beware, whose vain
Hydroptic soap my meagre water saves.
Male spiders must not be too early slain.

WILLIAM EMPSON (1906 – 84)   143

WEB-MAKING

A spider sways along that wondrous slur,
its own silk, thrown from columbine to undiscovered
columbine, and when the cat's moony head
destroys the suspension, the spider
levitates to another flower to loop, in the quiet,
something like a line drawing of a constellation,
botanical, feeling with its 8 legs
for the tensile strength, as the mind plays with
        theorems.

Sometimes the spider, small as a fingertip, as a star
        beyond one's finger,
on its silk swing swings up high
and winks away.

To study the spider and its web-making
you need a random sample of many
and a delicate telescope to watch the garden, the
        columbine.
They habitually spin at night.
Dawns you can feel their wet, invisible lines
cross your skin. That's when you notice
the apparent chasms they must cross, and think the
        natural world
and the quantum heaves of crab, ram & bear

are as the Ancients saw them in the mind's eye,
pulled most delicately
together by silk inventions. What is a web?

Something time takes to finish, or to break,
or to become the way things look in.

"A SPIDER SEWED AT NIGHT"

A Spider sewed at Night
Without a Light
Upon an Arc of White.

If Ruff it was of Dame
Or Shroud of Gnome
Himself himself inform.

Of Immortality
His Strategy
Was Physiognomy.

DESIGN

I found a dimpled spider, fat and white,
On a white heal-all, holding up a moth
Like a white piece of rigid satin cloth –
Assorted characters of death and blight
Mixed ready to begin the morning right,
Like the ingredients of a witches' broth –
A snow-drop spider, a flower like a froth,
And dead wings carried like a paper kite.

What had that flower to do with being white,
The wayside blue and innocent heal-all?
What brought the kindred spider to that height,
Then steered the white moth thither in the night?
What but design of darkness to appall? –
If design govern in a thing so small.

ROBERT FROST (1874–1963)   147

WHAT THE SPIDER HEARD

Will there be time for eggnogs and eclogues
In the place where we're going?
Said the spider to the fly.

    I think not, said the fly.
    I think not, sang the chorus.
    I think not, said a stranger
    Who mysteriously happened by.

Will they beat me and treat me the way they did here,
In the place where we're going?
Asked the spider of the fly.

    It is likely, said the fly.
    Very likely, sang the chorus.
    Extremely likely, said the stranger,
    With an eager gleam in his eye.

O, why go there when we know there is nothing there
      but fear
At this place where we're going?
Said the spider to the fly.

What a question! said the fly.
What a question! sang the chorus.
What a question! said the stranger,
Leering slightly at the spider,
Winking slyly at the fly.

THE SPIDER AND THE
GHOST OF THE FLY

Once I loved a spider
When I was born a fly,
A velvet-footed spider
With a gown of rainbow-dye.
She ate my wings and gloated.
She bound me with a hair.
She drove me to her parlor
Above her winding stair.
To educate young spiders
She took me all apart.
My ghost came back to haunt her.
I saw her eat my heart.

MR. EDWARDS AND THE SPIDER

I saw the spiders marching through the air,
Swimming from tree to tree that mildewed day
   In latter August when the hay
    Came creaking to the barn. But where
      The wind is westerly,
Where gnarled November makes the spiders fly
Into the apparitions of the sky,
They purpose nothing but their ease and die
Urgently beating east to sunrise and the sea;

What are we in the hands of the great God?
It was in vain you set up thorn and briar
   In battle array against the fire
    And treason crackling in your blood;
      For the wild thorns grow tame
And will do nothing to oppose the flame;
Your lacerations tell the losing game
You play against a sickness past your cure.
How will the hands be strong? How will the heart
   endure?

A very little thing, a little worm,
Or hourglass-blazoned spider, it is said,
   Can kill a tiger. Will the dead
    Hold up his mirror and affirm

To the four winds the smell
And flash of his authority? It's well
If God who holds you to the pit of hell,
   Much as one holds a spider, will destroy,
Baffle and dissipate your soul. As a small boy

On Windsor Marsh, I saw the spider die
When thrown into the bowels of fierce fire:
   There's no long struggle, no desire
   To get up on its feet and fly –
      It stretches out its feet
And dies. This is the sinner's last retreat;
Yes, and no strength exerted on the heat
Then sinews the abolished will, when sick
And full of burning, it will whistle on a brick.

But who can plumb the sinking of that soul?
Josiah Hawley, picture yourself cast
   Into a brick-kiln where the blast
   Fans your quick vitals to a coal –
      If measured by a glass,
How long would it seem burning! Let there pass
A minute, ten, ten trillion; but the blaze
Is infinite, eternal: this is death,
To die and know it. This is the Black Widow, death.

SPIDER

The spider can barely walk, his legs are so scared –
he's got to get from the bar of soap to the uppermost
showerstall tile that is his home, and he has suffered
a betrayal so great he's lost in his own neighborhood,
crawling on his hands and knees, so to speak,
    in and out
of the shadows of other tiles he's passed before but
barely recognizes, given his state of shock and
    disbelief.
Spiders don't hear very well – he can't hear the rain
as it falls and cools his flaming legs, the distant
    screams
of another's crisis mean nothing to him, he can't hear
his own heartbeat, an alarm casting his skeleton
    straight
into hell, his blood ignited by the bellows of loss.
If the gods implore him to hold his saliva, he doesn't
hear them, he goes on crawling toward the one
    safe spot,
which has become, in his mind, the destination of
    his life
and this night rolled into one, a wet bag at the bottom
of which, were it to fall, would lie his demise –
too awful to discuss.

MARY RUEFLE (1952 –)

IN WHICH A SPIDER WEAVES A WEB
ON MY COMPUTER SCREEN

1
What is that shadow that weaves itself so fine
across the edge of my computer screen?
There it is, a pinprick of a spider weaving
a web I'm looking through, as if it were a veil of
    second
sight that as I type these words behind
the veil, the screen-light shines right through.

It weaves the sun into its web and turns
the screen into a mirror reflecting
my own eyes looking at the spider
and wondering what the spider thinks of me.
Hello, pal, I want to say, but that feels
phony, too familiar for what I know

I'm going to do. The web sways
and ripples each time I breathe, getting ready
to rip it away. There's a lot of casual brutality
to reconcile. The spider clings to its web's outer rim,
plucks with a slender leg a near-invisible guywire
each time I type a word and the silk trembles.

2

He said that being a refugee was like living like a
    spider
in the bottom of a well. He held his quiet dignity
close to him. The others in the room stopped talking.

I won't repeat exactly what he said since it's his
to tell. But it had to do with how his mother died,
how his home was destroyed. The words you use

to talk about such things, the second they're
uttered, sound suspect. For him to say, *The soldiers
shot my father, they blew up our house, and the worst*

*thing I ever saw, the very worst, was seeing my baby
brother crying on my dead mother's breast*
is only my rendering in English what the translator

speaking in French said he said. Ravelled in
words as a spider is ravelled in its silk, I think
I should know what to want to say but to want

to say is not what the man in his use of a figure
of a spider drifting suspended, tethered
to a lifeline spinning out impossibly fine, intends

when he says, "The deeds to my house are stained
with blood" and then shows you the stains, three long
    stains
dried brown and fading above the signature line.

SPIDER

How you like these threads, said white spider
traveling back and forth between two rooms in
Lambertville, New Jersey, his web a work of
art, truly excessive, spit from his soul,
and the first case of any spit, it came from
my own soul since I am a mimic neurotic.
But how you like my steel? You like my window?
You like my big eye waiting? How you like my
chandelier? How you like fate? You like
my silk? Do cover your legs, do tighten
the arms a little, do tighten around the neck.
And how you like my kiss? How about
my rasping bloody tongue? Weren't those herbs
and such like any household, giant unkempt
Russian sage, the better to smell you, my dear,
and spicy rosemary beside the orange and
purple echinacea, all that a little
to placate – though I know you don't believe it,
for nature is nature – your perverted Isaiah
from running around like crazy in the meat markets.

GERALD STERN (1925 –)   157

A NOISELESS PATIENT SPIDER

A noiseless patient spider,
I mark'd where on a little promontory it stood
    isolated,
Mark'd how to explore the vacant vast surrounding,
It launch'd forth filament, filament, filament, out of
    itself,
Ever unreeling them, ever tirelessly speeding them.

And you O my soul where you stand,
Surrounded, detached, in measureless oceans of space,
Ceaselessly musing, venturing, throwing, seeking the
    spheres to connect them,
Till the bridge you will need be form'd, till the ductile
    anchor hold,
Till the gossamer thread you fling catch somewhere,
    O my soul.

HAIKU

24

The webs of spiders
Sticking to my sweaty face
In the dusty woods.

76

The path in the woods
Is barred by spider webs
Beaded with spring rain.

122

And what do *you* think,
O still and awesome spider,
Of this summer rain?

RICHARD WRIGHT (1908 – 60)

CRAWLERS

COCKROACH

the cockroach crouched
against the tile
while I was pissing and as
I turned my head
he hauled his butt
into a crack.
I got the can and sprayed
and sprayed and sprayed
and finally the roach came out
and gave me a very dirty look.
then he fell down into
the bathtub and I watched
him dying
with a subtle pleasure
because I paid the rent
and he didn't.
I picked him up with
some greenblue toilet
paper and flushed him
away. that's all there
was to that, except
around Hollywood and
Western we have to
keep doing it.
they say some day that

tribe is going to
inherit the earth
but we're going to
make them wait a
few months.

THE CATERPILLAR

The enormous green caterpillar,
nourished on rain
and on leaf-blood,
the giant caterpillar with its bristling hairs,
whose head is one great snout,
whose violet antennae
troubled the air –
the storm hurled it on my table
one early evening
when the cold came down,
obliging me to watch it
drag itself along, unconscious
of the threat it held for me,
but tenacious in its movement
toward me, the caterpillar
with its electric flesh,
that approached me with determined slowness,
entering forever
into my orbit,
fat, green, wet, and blind.

NINA CASSIAN (1924 – 2014)

NEW ORLEANS PALMETTO BUG

"We . . . feel a kiss on our lips
Trembling there like a small insect."
— ARTHUR RIMBAUD

1. False Gods

I'm terrified of the one
in my kitchen. It's as long as my index finger,
& two thumbs wide – so big, so
alive with its bigness, that I can't imagine
putting my foot on top & pressing –
anymore than I could imagine
pressing down
on a hummingbird or newborn kitten.
I'm screaming &
waving my hands, but it doesn't move. Then, slow
& steady, it starts to walk toward me. I'm yelling,
"You dumb ass, you stupid mother fucker." I'm so
big, so
powerful, I can't believe
it won't
obey me! "Ok," I say, this time
with assurance, "You better not
go in my bedroom," but it does the very thing
I told it not

to do, heads straight
down the hall, through my door & climbs up
on the heater
beside my bed. (Imagine
me trying to sleep & feeling
that slight tremble
on my lips!) I grab the heater
& carry it, carefully (I don't want to hurt
it when it falls!), out the front door
to the porch, begging, "Please, go home
to your own people." But it holds on,
as if it doesn't want to leave.

Later, as I'm drifting off,
I hear the long soft clickings
of a chorus
outside my window & I wonder
if it brought back
a bunch of its friends
to serenade me to sleep.

2. Why the giant palmetto bugs in New Orleans run
toward you when you are screaming at them to go away

They have a hard thing
on the top of their head that sticks out
like the bill of a baseball cap (but pointy),

so they can't
look up; they
only see the ground & don't know
you're screaming & waving
your hands. They only see
your foot & they imagine
its cool shadow: what a good place
to hide, they say.

THE ROACH

When the roach wriggled into my ear
It wriggled into my sleep, and in my dreams
I heard a damp drum, and woke.

My father had a house, but we were poor,
Poor meaning you slept where
Stuff could get at you.

My little insect brother found me asleep, and
    I guess we've
All stumbled upon what at first feels like luck;
Up the trail the pioneer walks, until winter buries

The short-cut ahead, and the road behind,
    which was now
The tale of a roach in a boy's ear. Those days,
I slept in the Living Room

With my shabby dad, he on one couch, me
On mine. I still think of his feet, sockless,
How oddly white they looked below his darker calf,
    how

I wanted to ask how, why, were you ever teased,
But being scared (though he never struck me) or
Too polite, the question stuck between my teeth and
    tongue.

It occurs to me now that the thrum that snapped open
My eyes were the roach's wings, useless as a hen's,
Pleading for flight, scratching for a window, or a door

Back to normal, the bread crumbs that missed
    my mother's
Dish rag, a delight of droppings in the pantry, and he
    buzzed in
My left ear, the jerky dance we do as the walls
    close in,

How he buzzed.

COCKROACH

Blackly armoured as a dictator's funeral,
arch-survivor so easily crushed by my foot,
you die as you lived, without expression,
squat body, fine carapace, fusing or sundering.

I know a further million of you wait –
the underground sea on which this house floats.
While I was gone, you tracked each plate, pot, cup,
dining on the ghosts of past meals; invaded
sealed crates of books, a ghostlier sustenance.

Moving with the illusion of slowness
then cannily absent, you often subvert, outwit.
Sometimes, I find you in dreams, or odd pockets
of the self – just there as if to say:
   I cannot be transformed, kill me or endure me.
   Remember, nothing describes me but what I am.
   And don't *write poems about me.*

DIANE FAHEY (1945 –)   171

THE CATERPILLAR

Under this loop of honeysuckle,
A creeping, coloured caterpillar,
I gnaw the fresh green hawthorn spray,
I nibble it leaf by leaf away.

Down beneath grow dandelions,
Daisies, old-man's-looking-glasses;
Rooks flap croaking across the lane.
I eat and swallow and eat again.

Here come raindrops helter-skelter;
I munch and nibble unregarding:
Hawthorn leaves are juicy and firm.
I'll mind my business: I'm a good worm.

When I'm old, tired, melancholy,
I'll build a leaf-green mausoleum
Close by, here on this lovely spray,
And die and dream the ages away.

Some say worms win resurrection,
With white wings beating flitter-flutter,
But wings or a sound sleep, why should I care?
Either way I'll not miss my share.

Under this loop of honeysuckle,
A hungry, hairy caterpillar,
I crawl on my high and swinging seat,
And eat, eat, eat – as one ought to eat.

THE GRUB

The almost transparent white grub moves
slowly along the edge of the frying pan.
The grease makes the only sound, loud
in the empty room. Even the rim is cooking him.
The worm stops. Raises his head slightly.
Lowers it, moving tentatively down the side.
He seems to be moving on his own time,
but he is falling by definition. He moves forward
touching the frying grease with his whole face.

THE VERY HUNGRY CATERPILLAR

After gluttony the insatiable rain

Drowns the earth and all the ruins
Remain cannot be finished off

You climb up to the highest post
A lemon tree

You become visible suspected at first
Of being bird excrement
Its odd landing

Visible through the kitchen window
Of all who can dislocate you from a leaf

To the concrete with a twig
And unsure what you believe

When jabbed when your red-horned tongue flashes
Out of your grotesque head

I poke you writhe
A green juice out of you the color

Of the earth you ravaged
Mint and thyme

The next day the sun
The rest of your clan
A festival on branches

Your cranium a Worf's
Your future a swallowtail

CENTIPEDE

That night, above the folds of the Aegean,
the coils of my body cool on *meltemia*'s whistle.
When razor pain inside the lip startles me awake,
I assume *dream*, perhaps the bite of some clean
leave-taking –

                but next to me, lithe and lava-dark
on the milky pillow, a curl, a loop of neglected
cursive, perfectly still.
I sweep it off. Small terror
gives way to disgust, then dissolves
as I cocoon in the heat of my husband's hold.
It must have meant no harm, primeval creature
whose ancestry puts mine to shame,
skimming stone crevices and bathroom drains,
then starched sheets, summoned
by heat and moisture toward my mouth.
When he wisps into bed the next, then another night,
his parceled body, once sewn with a hundred tales,
unthreads. He lends me pincers.
I unseal the ink of my lips.
By sunbreak, we've woven the first line of a new myth.

THE CATERPILLAR

Brown and furry
Caterpillar in a hurry;
Take your walk
To the shady leaf or stalk.

May no toad spy you,
May the little birds pass by you;
Spin and die,
To live again a butterfly.

ST. ROACH

For that I never knew you, I only learned to dread
      you,
for that I never touched you, they told me you are
      filth,
they showed me by every action to despise your kind;
for that I saw my people making war on you,
I could not tell you apart, one from another,
for that in childhood I lived in places clear of you,
for that all the people I knew met you by
crushing you, stamping you to death, they poured
      boiling water on you, they flushed you down,
for that I could not tell one from another
only that you were dark, fast on your feet, and slender.
   Not like me.
For that I did not know your poems
And that I do not know any of your sayings
And that I cannot speak or read your language
And that I do not sing your songs
And that I do not teach our children
          to eat your food
          or know your poems
          or sing your songs
But that we say you are filthing our food
But that we know you not at all.

Yesterday I looked at one of you for the first time.
You were lighter than the others in color, that was
    neither good nor bad.
I was really looking for the first time.
You seemed troubled and witty.

Today I touched one of you for the first time.
You were startled, you ran, you fled away
Fast as a dancer, light, strange and lovely to the touch.
I reach, I touch, I begin to know you.

DEATH OF A COCKROACH

I opened wide the bath-room door,
And all at once switched on the light,
When moving swift across the floor
I saw a streak of ebon bright:
Then quick, with slipper in my hand,
Before it could escape, – I slammed.
I missed it once, I missed it twice,
But got it ere it gained its lair.
I fear my words were far from nice,
Though d——s with me are rather rare:
Then lo! I thought that dying roach
Regarded me with some reproach.

Said I: "Don't think I grudge you breath;
I hate to spill your greenish gore,
But why did you invite your death
By straying on my bath-room floor?"
"It is because," said he (or she),
"Adventure is my destiny.

"By evolution I was planned,
And marvellously made as you;
And I am led to understand
The selfsame God conceived us two:

Sire, though the coup de grâce you give,
Even a roach has right to live."

Said I: "Of course you have a right, –
But not to blot my bath-room floor.
Yet though with slipper I may smite,
Your doom I morally deplore . . .
From cellar gloom to stellar space
Let bards and beetles have their place."

COCKROACH

Roach, foulest of creatures,
who attacks with yellow teeth
and an army of cousins big as shoes,
you are lumps of coal that are mechanized
and when I turn on the light you scuttle
into the corners and there is this hiss upon the land.
Yet I know you are only the common angel
turned into, by way of enchantment, the ugliest.
Your uncle was made into an apple.
Your aunt was made into a Siamese cat,
all the rest were made into butterflies
but because you lied to God outrightly –
told him that all things on earth were in order –
He turned his wrath upon you and said,
I will make you the most loathsome,
I will make you into God's lie,
and never will a little girl fondle you
or hold your dark wings cupped in her palm.

But that was not true. Once in New Orleans
with a group of students a roach fled across
the floor and I shrieked and she picked it up
in her hands and held it from my fear for one hour.
And held it like a diamond ring that should not
        escape.

These days even the devil is getting overturned
and held up to the light like a glass of water.

COCKROACH

When I see a cockroach,
I don't grow violent like you.
I stop as if a friendly greeting
Had passed between us.

*

This roach is familiar to me.
We met here and there,
In the kitchen at midnight,
And now on my pillow.

*

I can see it has a couple
Of my black hairs
Sticking out of its head,
And who knows what else?

*

It carries false papers —
Don't ask me how I know.
False papers, yes,
With my greasy thumbprint.

CHARLES SIMIC (1938 –)   185

LORD COCKROACH

Near-dead roaches seem enraptured in prayer,
Rocking their sleek sheaths, papery coffins,
As they tease out one leg, then another,
Uncoil a copper antenna, summon
Roachy gods.
    Their dying takes forever,
So they hospice themselves on the bathroom's
Honeycombed tiles, dun husks swaddled in dust,
The young lucent as crinkled cellophane,
The two-inch ancients umber shades darker
In their wooden boats, woolen overcoats,
Wings like shrouds carted across continents –
Who fled the sudden light-flood, fled again
The thunderous, percussive lovemaking
In a time of famine, a time of war.
Their dying takes forever, so I bear
Each body with tender care in crumpled
Tissue, then let fall the brittle faithful
Into still waters quickly flushed.
       Their gods

Must think they're witnessing ceremony,
One more ritual in a roach-ruled world
To remind myself, my wary lover
Ill with disgust beneath plush bedcovers,
How on six wiry legs
                     Death
                         approaches.

MICHAEL WATERS (1949 –)   187

STINGERS, BITERS,
AND SUCKERS

MOSQUITOES

At first the hum through sagging leaves
seemed less like engines,
more like the night's mosquitoes come early.
It seemed that close. All spring
the rains had fallen, grass and weeds growing
burly in the parks. Buried in the mud,
born there, the swarms rose
and sprinkled each evening's air,
slow in the last light, but wild by bedtime,
biting whatever would bleed.

At first the hum seemed more like that.
I brushed the hair at my ears,
waving to no one in the humid dusk.
And then that cloud, beautifully
white in the falling dark, simply lifted
out of the trees, still blocks away.
I watched it move like slow fog closer.
The old porch trellis shook by its vines
by the time the truck turned
the last corner and roared down the street,

spraying in great billows for mosquitoes.
For hours, it seemed, the pale
fog stayed in the air, clinging like cobwebs

to the still leaves, sifting finally
up into stars. And when I tried to sleep,
sheets kicked off, it's true,
nothing batted the window-screens.
But something wanted me just the same,
or seemed to, hovering there:
around my ears, blocks away, circling.

BY THE POOL

By the pool,
we hear them buzzing,
drinking in the honey from our tea,

scent of our suntan lotion. The nest
in the corner of our side table where they breed
seemingly light as a harmless ball of cotton,

a colony of yellow jackets – one
to two thousand waiting –

to anoint the queen.

JILL BIALOSKY (1957–)

THE FLEA

Marke but this flea, and marke in this,
How little that which thou deny'st me is;
It suck'd me first, and now sucks thee,
And in this flea, our two bloods mingled bee;
Thou know'st that this cannot be said
A sinne, nor shame, nor losse of maidenhead,
    Yet this enjoyes before it wooe,
      And pamper'd swells with one blood made of two,
      And this, alas, is more than wee would doe.

Oh stay, three lives in one flea spare,
Where wee almost, yea more than maryed are.
This flea is you and I, and this
Our mariage bed, and mariage temple is;
Though parents grudge, and you, w'are met,
And cloysterd in these living walls of Jet.
    Though use make you apt to kill mee,
      Let not to that, selfe murder added bee,
      And sacrilege, three sinnes in killing three.

Cruell and sodaine, hast thou since
Purpled thy naile, in blood of innocence?
Wherein could this flea guilty bee,
Except in that drop which it suckt from thee?
Yet thou triumph'st, and saist that thou

Find'st not thy selfe, nor mee the weaker now;
    'Tis true, then learne how false, feares bee;
    Just so much honor, when thou yeeld'st to mee,
Will wast, as this flea's death tooke life from thee.

GNAT ON MY PAPER

He has two antennae,
They search back and forth,
Left and right, up and down.

He has four feet,
He is exploring what I write now.

This is a living being,
Is this a living poem?

His life is a quarter of an inch.
I could crack him any moment now.

Now I see he has two more feet,
Almost too delicate to examine.

He is still sitting on this paper,
An inch away from An.

Does he know who I am,
Does he know the importance of man?

He does not know or sense me,
His antennae are still sensing.

I wonder if he knows it is June,
The world in its sensual height?

How absurd to think
That he never thought of Plato.

He is satisfied to sit on this paper,
For some reason he has not flown away.

Small creature, gnat on my paper,
Too slight to be given a thought,

I salute you as the evanescent,
I play with you in my depth.

What, still here? Still evanescent?
You are my truth, that vanishes.

Now I put down this paper,
He has flown into the infinite.
He could not say it.

RICHARD EBERHART (1904–2005)   197

"FLEAS INTEREST ME SO MUCH"

Fleas interest me so much
that I let them bite me for hours.
They are perfect, ancient, Sanskrit,
machines that admit of no appeal.
They do not bite to eat,
they bite only to jump;
they are the dancers of the celestial sphere,
delicate acrobats
in the softest and most profound circus;
let them gallop on my skin,
divulge their emotions,
amuse themselves with my blood,
but someone should introduce them to me.
I want to know them closely,
I want to know what to rely on.

TRANSLATED BY ELSA NEUBERGER

MOSQUITOES

When my father wanted to point out galaxies
or Andromeda or the Seven Sisters, I'd complain
of the huzz of mosquitoes, or of the yawning
moon-quiet in that slow, summer air. All I wanted

was to go inside into our cooled house and watch TV
or paint my nails. What does a fifteen-year-old girl
know of patience? What did I know of the steady turn
of whole moon valleys cresting into focus?

Standing there in our driveway with him,
I smacked my legs, my arms, and my face
while I waited for him to find whatever pinhole
of light he wanted me to see. At night, when I washed

my face, I'd find bursts of blood and dried bodies
slapped into my skin. Complaints at breakfast about
how I'd never do it again, how I have more homework
now, Dad. How I can't go to school with bites all over

my face anymore, Dad.   Now – I hardly
ever say no. He has plans to go star-gazing
with his grandson and for once, I don't protest.
He has plans. I know one day he won't ask me,

won't be there to show me the rings of Saturn
glowing gold through the eyepiece. He won't be there
to show me how the moons of Jupiter jump
if you catch them on a clear night. I know

one day I will look up into the night sky
searching, searching — I know the mosquitoes
will still have their way with me —
and my father won't hear me complain.

MOSQUITOES

They are born in the swamps of sleeplessness.
They are a viscous blackness which wings about.
Little frail vampires,
miniature dragonflies,
small picadors
with the devil's own sting.

JOSÉ EMILIO PACHECO (1939 – 2014)   201
TRANSLATED BY ALASTAIR REID

WASPS' NEST

It was the fruit I wanted, not the nest.
The nest was hanging like the richest fruit
against the sun. I took the nest

and with it came the heart, and in my hand
the kingdom and the queen, frail surfaces,
rested for a moment. Then the drones

awoke and did their painful business.
I let the city drop upon the stones.
It split to its deep palaces and combs.

It bled the insect gold,
the pupa queens like tiny eyes
wriggled from their sockets, and somewhere

the monarch cowered in a veil of wings
in passages through which at evening
the labourers had homed,

burdened with silence and the garden scents.
The secret heart was broken suddenly.
I, to whom the knowledge had been given,

who was not after knowledge but a fruit,
remember how a knot of pains
swelled my hand to a round nest;

blood throbbed in the hurt veins
as if an unseen swarm mined there.
The nest oozed bitter honey.

I swaddled my fat hand in cotton.
After a week pain gave it back to me
scarred and weakened like a shrivelled skin.

A second fruit is growing on the tree.
Identical – the droning in the leaves.
It ripens. I have another hand.

THE WASP

Where the ripe pears droop heavily
   The yellow wasp hums loud and long
   His hot and drowsy autumn song:
A yellow flame he seems to be,
   When darting suddenly from high
   He lights where fallen peaches lie:

Yellow and black, this tiny thing's
A tiger-soul on elfin wings.

ASK THE LOCALS

Nobody knows: How those so-called revolutionaries
who wanted so-called Year Zero so bad,
turned into mosquitoes. I mean, mosquitoes, right?
Because not butterflies or moths rolling
in the mass graves – we all know the moths are
        children
who didn't make it past five. My theory is those creeps
suck the blood of their victims to forget
with their bare hands or with other kinds of hands,
the kinds with teeth. They forgot. Don't forget: If you
scratch your arms like that, a huge welt will appear –
a rash, and those mosquitoes will keep coming.
You heard it from me. Don't scratch their real names.
Toothpaste over that bump won't soothe you,
not this one. I'll tell you something personal:
        Every time
I hear their real names, I itch my skin. I itch my
        own name
too. *Mosquitoes.* Call them *mosquitoes.* This kind keeps
        going
like that mosquito's straw on your calf keeps sucking.
This is when I tell you: Don't bend.
Slap.

UPON A WASP CHILD WITH COLD

The Bare that breaths the Northern blast
Did numb, Torpedo like, a Wasp
Whose stiffend limbs encrampt, lay bathing
In Sol's warm breath and shine as saving,
Which with her hands she chafes and stands
Rubbing her Legs, Shanks, Thighs, and hands.
Her petty toes, and fingers ends
Nipt with this breath, she out extends
Unto the Sun, in greate desire
To warm her digits at that fire.
Doth hold her Temples in this state
Where pulse doth beate, and head doth ake.
Doth turn, and stretch her body small,
Doth Comb her velvet Capitall.
As if her little brain pan were
A Volume of Choice precepts cleare.
As if her sattin jacket hot
Contained Apothecaries Shop
Of Natures recepts, that prevails
To remedy all her sad ailes,
As if her velvet helmet high
Did turret rationality.
She fans her wing up to the Winde
As if her Pettycoate were lin'de,
With reasons fleece, and hoises sails

And hu'ming flies in thankfull gails
Unto her dun Curld palace Hall
Her warm thanks offering for all.

Lord cleare my misted sight that I
May hence view thy Divinity.
Some sparkes whereof thou up dost hasp
Within this little downy Wasp
In whose small Corporation wee
A school and a schoolmaster see
Where we may learn, and easily finde
A nimble Spirit bravely minde
Her worke in e'ry limb: and lace
It up neate with a vitall grace,
Acting each part though ne'er so small
Here of this Fustian animall.
Till I enravisht Climb into
The Godhead on this Lather doe.
Where all my pipes inspir'de upraise
An Heavenly musick furrd with praise.

AEDES AEGYPTI

With the audio on *mute*, the television
flickers over the bodies of lovers
tangled in dream, carbon dioxide
pluming from their mouths
the way factory smoke billows
from the industrial park outside of town.

Mosquitoes circle in a holding pattern above.
As the female's wings beat 400 times
per second, the male's at 600 hertz,
their wingtips trace the smallest figure-8s
into the invisible, a gesture toward the infinite.

Such brief lives they have. One month,
maybe, their coupling a conversation
at 1200 hertz, the high pitch of their union
an *A* above concert *C* –

      Beethoven's last note,
perhaps, the note he chose not to take
by feather from the well of ink
the way a mosquito might dip a stylet
in blood.

He let the note play itself out.
To recognize the cry of the bat
with its hunger returning. Blue notes
smoldered out from the throats of lovers.
That no matter how certain
the crushing weight of the indomitable,
even the smallest of flyers
raise their wings in music.

SWEET BLOOD

Like stars the mosquitoes
swarm. He's gone. We sit

unscreened on the porch,
my father doused

in bugspray, that sweet-sick
stank. We drink

because my father's father be buried,
because the road will not carry

anyone but cousins, or neighbors
whose silhouettes and dust

we know. We drink.
Only son of an only son,

I do not share
my father's sweet blood –

what draws the skeeters
near him, braving the repellent

cloud, his quick hands, for a taste.
Finally my father gives –

I'm getting eaten up –
and heads inside

slapping red his legs.
Somewhere by the highwayside

my grandfather rests, his body
vaulted in ground that does not shift

we hope, or give back its dead.
We drink and forgive

the bugs who come for us
with dusk, who draw blood

the way we swallow
thin beer and words

like *love* – in order
to survive.

PESTS

FLIES

The story goes that as a boy,
the great Polish writer Bruno Schulz
fed sugar water to the last houseflies of autumn,
giving them strength for the bitter winter.
And I read about another lover of *Musca domestica*
who with only a whistle and the force of concentration
taught one envoy to come to his desk.
It would orbit, then land on his wrist
with a minute impact. Then they could reflect together,
the insect with his complex eye, the man, his simple one.
I am a novice with many failures,
but if the day is cool enough I can capture
a compliant fly in clear glass,
all emerald thorax and buzzing wings,
releasing it into the afternoon.
And by night I've perfected a method
for shepherding strays out to the stars.
Starting with the farthest room in my home,
I extinguish the lamps one by one,
luring the flies from dark to bright.
When I reach the door with my small skein,
I illumine the porch light, open the screen,
and watch them sail out from the shadows
into the warm yellow current.

ELLEN BASS (1947–)

FRUIT FLIES

At the bottom of the jar, an apple core
floating in vinegar. At the bottom of the vinegar,
the dead. I grip the lip and the two of us look in

from opposite sides. The round door of the funnel
remains open, open in exactly the same place.
Can they not see this? Or can they just not,

by some curse of anatomy, crawl or fly
back out the way they came? That their lives
go from egg to adult in eight days

pains me. Before this apartment, before
these fruit flies that rise from the throat of our sink
and plague each glass of wine we raise,

we used to take apples to the cemetery off campus
and if the ground was dry, lie on the grassy path
between the rows. Beneath the fall sky,

we sucked dark doors into each other's skin.
We widened the wound of each other.
You had poems taped to your wall, as did I.

THE FLY

Little Fly,
Thy summer's play
My thoughtless hand
Has brush'd away.

Am not I
A fly like thee?
Or art not thou
A man like me?

For I dance,
And drink, & sing,
Till some blind hand
Shall brush my wing.

WILLIAM BLAKE (1757–1827)   217

THE HORSEFLY

A small kamikaze
knocks itself out against the window.
The morning chill might have
awoken him from the night's bacchanal
— we too
needed to shut the windows
and hurry to cover ourselves
because of the sudden storm —
and now (a bit more punk
than Baudelaire's albatross)
the stunned horsefly resigns
his elusive elegance.

FABIÁN CASAS (1965 —)
TRANSLATED BY ADRIANA SCOPINO

THE HOST

While I have been away the fruit flies
have moved in with their extended family
and rise politely off a feast of black
banana skin to welcome me home. I swat
and slap, but they just laugh on the updraft
of my flapping, batting hands.

The banana gone, I open a window,
hoping they will make off to some other repast
but they post a halo round my head,
two hundred wingbeats to a second, hatched
with a brain far quicker than mine. At my desk,
I am possessed, follow the threads for evidence

of pestilence, the death of civilisations
by Zebub, Arob, all the dust of Egypt
turned to gnats that torment livestock, squat
on ruined crop, rotted fish and frog.
In the face of this invasion, I am
an avenger sent to stop a plague,

enter *Kill Fruit Flies*, study the traps, fill
a glass jar with cider vinegar, stir in sugar,
cover with cunning cling-film, pierce and wait,
and they come, hover like decorous guests

at a table, perch on the rim. I watch them drown
one by one, then return to my desk. But just

as I begin to write, one rises up at the edge
of my sight like the crop-duster in North
by Northwest. I spin back into battle, set
the trap again, more delicious, more sugar, more
stealth. It sits on the lip, licks at the cling-film,
sips. I strike. It dies a vinegar death.

Through the rest of the day I revisit the site.
No sign of return. The next morning no-one
is there, the jar untouched, my table bare
in the desolate kitchen. I try to work but keep
coming back to stand like an expectant host
waiting to welcome the guest I miss.

THE FLY

How large unto the tiny fly
  Must little things appear! —
A rosebud like a feather bed,
  Its prickle like a spear;

A dewdrop like a looking-glass,
  A hair like golden wire;
The smallest grain of mustard-seed
  As fierce as coals of fire;

A loaf of bread, a lofty hill;
  A wasp, a cruel leopard;
And specks of salt as bright to see
  As lambkins to a shepherd.

WALTER DE LA MARE (1873—1956)

"I HEARD A FLY BUZZ – WHEN I DIED"

I heard a Fly buzz – when I died –
The Stillness in the Room
Was like the Stillness in the Air –
Between the Heaves of Storm –

The Eyes around – had wrung them dry –
And Breaths were gathering firm
For that last Onset – when the King
Be witnessed – in the Room –

I willed my Keepsakes – Signed away
What portion of me be
Assignable – and then it was
There interposed a Fly –

With Blue – uncertain stumbling Buzz –
Between the light – and me –
And then the Windows failed – and then
I could not see to see –

LUAM & THE FLIES
— umbertide, asmara, new york, october, 2013

It was the end of the world.
The world was ending. I sat

in my house with the flies. Though
the night was dense, was long, we

tried to wait for light, to last.
But the wind at the doors. &

darkness knuckled, flashed its teeth.
Outside, the other houses,

outside, the solitary
field, tall singularity

of the mama tree. What was
strong was razed, what was alone.

I thought we would, plural, survive.
But I saw the deaths of flies.

I watched them clean their wings &
faces, then die in the night,

watching quietly out &,
looking, facing it. Morning

I saw them at the windows
as though remembering the

green, last world. Their legs curled in
the syllable of struggle,

or sleep. I counted six awes
who died in the night, whose sounds

died in degrees. Trying to learn,
I picked them gently up by

their wings & studied, then placed
the six onto one, white plate:

six corpses or comas, six
I tried to see but took to

the window & poured them out
for the dirt & rosemary.

   If I were moored to place, if
I had believed that this would

always be my home, if I
were to be lucky. One day

their descendants would be mine,
would handle my death, too, with

their small legs, yellow mouths &
wound-hungers. Powerless to

brush them from my teeth & eyes,
I'd be bright finally with

their taking, a city of
eggs, a harvest, an "&"; oh,

emerald signage of bodies.
I would be a kind of port

or harbor – Finally, them
again.

AMERICAN SONNET FOR MY PAST
AND FUTURE ASSASSIN

Why are you bugging me you stank minuscule husk
Of musk, muster & deliberation crawling over reasons
And possessions I have & have not touched?
Should I fail in my insecticide, I pray for a black boy
Who lifts you to a flame with bedeviled tweezers
Until mercy rises & disappears. You are the size
Of a stuttering drop of liquid — milk, machine oil
Semen, blood. Yes, you funky stud, you are the jewel
In the knob of an elegant butt plug, snug between
Pleasure & disgust. You are the scent of rot at the
        heart
Of love-making. The meat inside your exoskeleton
Is as tender as Jesus. Neruda wrote of "a nipple
Perfuming the earth." Yes, you are an odor, an almost
Imperceptible ode to death, a lousy, stinking stinkbug.

RESTLESS IN SPRING

Do not aspire to be a carefree mayfly
The mayfly lives just one day

And it might not be a good day
despite the sincere wishes
of the other mayflies
It might be black of sky with
pounding rain and birds
of relentless hunger

So you might consider moving on
and becoming a june bug
buried in the mud and secure
with your seventy loving eggs
until light penetrates the dark
and shrivels you up

What now? There are no
July bugs – You might
just try staying human

ROBERT HERSHON (1936 –)   227

BUZZ IN THE WINDOW

Buzz frantic
And prolonged. Fly down near the corner,
The cemetery den. A big blue-fly
Is trying to drag a plough, too deep
In earth too stony, immovable. Then the fly
Buzzing its full revs forward, budges backward.
Clings. Deadlock.
The spider has gripped its anus. Slender talons
Test the blue armour gently, the head
Buried in the big game. He tugs
Tigerish, half the size of his prey. A pounding
Glory-time for the spider. For the other
A darkening summary of some circumstances
In the window-corner, with a dead bee,
Wing-petals, husks of insect-armour, a brambled
Glade of dusty web. It buzzes less
As the drug argues deeper and deeper.
In fluttery soundless tremors it tries to keep
A hold on the air. The North sky
Moves northward. The blossom is clinging
To its hopes, re-furnishing the constant
Of ignorant life. The blue-fly,
Without changing expression, only adjusting
Its leg-stance, as if to more comfort,
Undergoes ultimate ghastliness. Finally agrees to it.

The spider tugs, retreating. The fly
Is going to let it do everything. Something is stuck.
The fly is fouled in web. Intelligence, the spider,
Comes round to look and patiently, joyfully,
Starts cutting the mesh. Frees it. Returns
To the haul – homeward in that exhausted ecstasy
The loaded hunters of the Pleistocene
Never recorded either.

TED HUGHES (1930−98)

FEVA

I was trying fo do my homework,
was hard fo concentrate, but.
I had one feva and one head cold.
Must have been going around
cuz my friend told me
get pleny students stay out sick.

I was getting dizzy, so I wen walk back to bed.
Befo I wen lie down, I pass my window
and saw da red ginger by da grass.
So nice. Ho, my head floating.
Man, would be nice if I can float
out da window fo pick up some red ginger, yeah?

I gotta sit down. Wen you sick, easy fo notice any kine
    stuff.
Like all da pukas in da screen window.
I wen even find one termite stay trapped inside da
    screen.
Poor ting, yeah? No mo wings. Look like one worm
just trying fo get in and nobody wen notice.
Nobody care about one termite.
Sad yeah, if nobody care about wat happen to you.
Den, you gotta take care yourself.
Lucky ting I get family.

I lie down and look at da ceiling.
Wat if I neva have one family?
I know some people no mo family
and life hard fo dem.
Lucky ting everybody still get dea healt.
Lucky ting all I get is one feva and head cold.
I close my eyes and da dizziness go away
and I fall into one deep sleep.

ANN INOSHITA (1970 –)

THE FLY

1
The fly
I've just brushed
from my face keeps buzzing
about me, flesh-
eater
starved for the soul.

One day I may learn to suffer
his mizzling, sporadic stroll over eyelid and cheek,
even be glad of his burnt singing.

2
The bee is beautiful.
She is the fleur-de-lis in the flesh.
She has a tuft of the sun on her back.
She brings sexual love to the narcissus flower.
She sings of fulfillment only
and stings and dies.
And everything she ever touches
is opening! opening!

And yet we say our last goodbye
to the fly last,
the flesh-fly last,
the absolute last,
the naked dirty reality of him last.

GALWAY KINNELL (1927 – 2014)

FLIES

You, familiar houseflies,
relentless gluttons,
common vulgar flies,
bring back everything.

O old voracious flies
like April bees,
old flies traipsing
over my childhood scalp!

Flies of my first boredom
in the family parlor
on shiny summer afternoons
when I started to dream!

And in that hated schoolroom
funny zooming flies
going after each other
with love for what flits —

everything flies — buzzing,
banging on the windowpanes
in autumn days . . .
Houseflies of all day long,

of childhood and adolescence,
of my golden youth,
of a second innocence
when I believed in nothing

forever . . . Ordinary flies,
the kind you always see,
won't come up with a fine tenor.
I know you've landed

ANTONIO MACHADO (1875–1939)
TRANSLATED BY WILLIS BARNSTONE

TO A TROUBLESOME FLY

What! here again, indomitable pest!
  Thou plagu'st me like a pepper-temper'd sprite;
  Thou makest me the butt of all thy spite,
And bitest me, and buzzest as in jest.
  Ten times I've closed my heavy lids in vain
This early morn to court an hour of sleep;
For thou – tormentor! – constantly dost keep
  Thy whizzing tones resounding through my brain,
Or lightest on my sensitive nose, and there
Thou trimm'st thy wings and shak'st thy legs of hair:
  Ten times I've raised my hand in haste to smite,
But thou art off; and ere I lay my head
And fold mine arms in quiet on my bed,
  Thou com'st again – and tak'st another bite.

As Uncle Toby says, "The world is wide
  Enough for thee and me."   Then go, I pray,
  And through this world do take some other way,
And let us travel no more side by side.
  Go, live among the flowers; go anywhere;
Or to the empty sugar-hogshead go,
That standeth at the grocer's store below;
  Go suit thy taste with any thing that's there.
There's his molasses-measure; there's his cheese,
And ham and herring: – What! will nothing please?

Presumptuous imp! then die! – But no! I'll smite
Thee not; for thou, perchance, art young in days,
And rather green as yet in this world's ways;
    So live and suffer – age may set thee right.

THE ROSE BEETLE

It is said that you came from China
but you never saw China
you eat up the leaves here

your ancestors travelled blind in eggs
you arrive just after dark from underground
with a clicking whir in the first night
knowing by the smell what leaves to eat here
where you have wakened for the first time

the strawberry leaves foreign as you
the beans the orchid tree the eggplant
the old leaves of the heliconia the banana some palms
and the roses from everywhere but here
and the hibiscus from here the abutilons
the royal ilima

in the night you turn them into lace
into an arid net
into sky

like the sky long ago over China

CLEGS AND MIDGES

1

The fact that Socrates is represented by Aristophanes
as a gadfly tormenting the body politic in some
     political horse-barn or byre
only stiffens

my resolve to raise the bar
back at the milking parlor. Taking their name from
     the Viking
term for a "burr,"

clegs have a way of spiking
a story whilst splashing it all over the front page.
I'll be damned if I'll let them come within striking

distance of my home patch.
The green of the cesspool is the green of ceremonial
     grade *matcha*.
Having made a botch

of my exposed forearms, the clegs now mooch
about the hindquarters of a heifer.
The bullock that had long since seemed to have lost
     his mojo

takes off across the water meadow like a zephyr.
Since I am no longer wont
to be targeted as Chilon the Ephor

was targeted by his fellow Spartans, when it comes to
    sustaining wounds
the clegs and I are pretty much even-steven.
The midges, in the meantime, have thrown caution to
    the winds.

2
The fact that Christ himself would seem to have
    suffered not only the ordeal
of a cleg in the side but a midge-coronet
is enough to rattle

the best of us. The purple of Jesus's robe is so
    ingrained
I may find it difficult to commit, in my new version, to
    Matthew's "scarlet."
I should be able to organize a workaround

in the matter of paying off the "harlot."
There'll be no stopping the presses. That's one of the
    translator's perks.
I'll be damned if I'll allow those varlets

to confine me to barracks
like the monk who offered me *matcha* in the Ryoan-ji
    temple in Kyoto.
The description of Saint Paul "kicking against the
    pricks"

I've chosen to render as "kicking against the *goads*"
so as not to offend any shrinking violets
among the money-lenders. I'm not going to dress up
    "a den of iniquity,"

though, when it comes to the playing of skin flutes.
I'm happy to go with the flow
particularly if the story stays below the fold,

given how a warble-fly
in the ointment is sometimes perceived by the *hoi
    polloi* as a major hurdle,
as if it represents some kind of character flaw.

3
The fact that a rabble tends to rouse the rabble
is no less true of our raised bogs
than the Boulevard Saint-Germain. It's only another
    ripple that sends the ripple

across a stagnant ring over which the midges box
so clever. My horse tugs at her halter
as if they've set their beaks

at her rather than me. Even the monk illuminating my
        version of the Psalter
views this world in terms of the column inch.
I'll be damned, too, if I'll falter

before the invisible. If the idea of a garden where
        everything seems to hinge
on one of its fifteen boulders
always being hidden from view sends a shiver through
        my palfrey's haunch,

it also makes my own unease look paltry.
It's true, of course, that Saint Patrick's claim to have
        herded swine on Slemish
connects him to Saint Anthony, another consensus-
        builder,

but the recent implanting of a microchip containing
        the entire Rhemish
Testament under the skin of my mare
confirms I'd not let a blemish

even slightly mar
my ambition. *Incorporate*, I always say, as a monk
    incorporates the hole of a warble
on a sheet of vellum into the phrase "less is m( )re."

ON A FLY DRINKING OUT OF HIS CUP

Busy, curious, thirsty fly!
Drink with me and drink as I:
Freely welcome to my cup,
Couldst thou sip and sip it up:
Make the most of life you may,
Life is short and wears away.

Both alike are mine and thine
Hastening quick to their decline:
Thine's a summer, mine's no more,
Though repeated to threescore.
Threescore summers, when they're gone,
Will appear as short as one!

244   WILLIAM OLDYS (1687–1761)

FLIES

This is the day the flies fall awake mid-sentence
and lie stunned on the window-sill shaking with
     speeches
only it isn't speech it is trembling sections of
     puzzlement which
break off suddenly as if the questioner had been shot

this is one of those wordy days
when they drop from their winter quarters in the
     curtains and sizzle as they fall
feeling like old cigarette butts called back to life
blown from the surface of some charred world

and somehow their wings which are little more than
     flakes of dead skin
have carried them to this blackened disembodied
     question

what dirt shall we visit today?
what dirt shall we re-visit?

they lift their faces to the past and walk about a bit
trying out their broken thought-machines
coming back with their used-up words

there is such a horrible trapped buzzing wherever
    we fly
it's going to be impossible to think clearly now until
    next winter
what should we
what dirt should we

COLD FLY

Noted outside the window: a fly, the sun on his back,
rubbing his legs together, relishing the morning
    brightness.
Sun and shadow about to shift – already he knows it,
suddenly flies off, to hum by a different window.

YANG WAN-LI (1127–1206)   247
TRANSLATED BY BURTON WATSON

ACKNOWLEDGMENTS

Thanks are due to the following copyright holders for permission to reprint:

DAVID BAKER: "Mosquitoes" from *Haunts*. Copyright © 1985 by David Baker. Reprinted with the permission of The Permissions Company, LLC on behalf of the Cleveland State University Poetry Center. ELLEN BASS: "Flies" from *Like a Beggar*. Copyright © 2014 by Ellen Bass. Reprinted with the permission of The Permissions Company, LLC on behalf of Copper Canyon Press, coppercanyonpress.org. GABRIELLE BATES: "Fruit Flies". Copyright © by Gabrielle Bates. Reprinted with permission from the poet. FIONA BENSON: "Blue Ghost Firefly". Reprinted with permission from the poet. JILL BIALOSKY: "XCVI. By the pool" from *Asylum: A Personal, Historical, Natural Inquiry in 103 Lyric Sections* by Jill Bialosky, copyright © 2020 by Jill Bialosky. Used by permission of Alfred A. Knopf, an imprint of the Knopf Doubleday Publishing Group, a division of Penguin Random House LLC. All rights reserved. Reprinted with permission of the Wylie Agency. ELIZABETH BISHOP: "Sleeping on the Ceiling" from *The Complete Poems 1927–1979*, reprinted with the permission of Farrar, Straus & Giroux and Chatto & Windus. LOUISE BOGAN: "The Dragonfly" from *Blue Estuaries*, Farrar, Straus & Giroux, 1995. Reprinted with the permission of Farrar, Straus & Giroux. KURT BROWN: "Bombing the Swarm" from *Return of the Prodigals*. Copyright © 1999 by Kurt Brown. Reprinted with the permission of The Permissions Company, LLC on behalf of Four Way Books, fourwaybooks.com. DAVID BUDBILL: "Bugs in a Bowl" from *Moment to Moment: Poems of a Mountain Recluse*. Copyright © 1999 by David Budbill. Reprinted with the permission of The Permissions Company, LLC on behalf of Copper Canyon Press, coppercanyonpress.org. CHARLES BUKOWSKI: "Cockroach" from *Love is a Dog from Hell: Poems 1974–1977*, HarperCollins